The Gen-X Cheat Codes for Retirement Income

Donte Ormsby

NEWHAVYN
PUBLISHING

NewHavyn Publishing

Contents

1. Start Here   1

2. CHEAT CODE 1: Master This Before You Go Forward   11

3. CHEAT CODE 2: The Art of Self-Duplication   24

4. CHEAT CODE 3: Your Hidden Leverage   34

5. CHEAT CODE 4: The $100 Test   45

6. CHEAT CODE 5: The Economy of Attention   55

7. CHEAT CODE 6: The Self-Duplication Playbook   66

8. CHEAT CODE 7: The Entropy Principle   78

9. CHEAT CODE 8: Plugging the Leak   90

10. CHEAT CODE 9: 401K Mysteries Solved   104

11. CHEAT CODE 10: Infinite Liquidity   119

12. WHATEVER   140

Start Here

Generation X. I remember when adults started referring to us under this moniker. "The Slacker Generation," they would say, with the slightest of sneers on their face—or was I imagining it?

They never knew what to make of us. We were respectful, but yet we were rebels. Contrary to popular belief, we were not slackers. We worked very hard. We simply never quite believed that the world worked the way our parents and mentors described. You know, devote your working life existence to a company and they will reward you someday with a generous pension and retirement plan... yeah, right.

Turns out our skepticism held up a little better than the advice.

And despite being faced our entire adult lives with the tongue-in-cheek, smirky comments Baby Boomers made about Social Security not being there for us when we need it, we still pressed on.

And now, here we are. Looking down the barrel of a gun called retirement. Some of us closer than others, but most of us agreeing it's a lot closer than we'd like to believe we're prepared for.

And that's where this book comes in.

Gen Xers have always been pretty good at taking care of ourselves. It started with latch-key afternoons, figuring out our homework on our own, and making our own snacks until some kind of adult got home. Turns out we're probably going to need to figure out retirement on our own too.

If you're okay with the thought of putting in a little creative work today, you can certainly help your retirement-self by creating some income streams that you'll be thankful for when your work years are over.

What This Book Is (And Isn't)

Let's be clear from the start: **This is not a traditional retirement planning book.**

You won't find complicated investment strategies, detailed break-downs of 401(k) contribution limits, or lectures about what you should have done twenty years ago. If you want that, there are plenty of books written by financial advisors in suits who've never missed a paycheck.

Genyus References

Throughout this book, you'll see the word "Genyus" used frequently—this is not a misspelling, but a reference to my company, Genyus Labs, which creates products and resources designed to help you succeed; visit Genyusmind.com to discover more tools for your financial journey.

This book is different.

This book is about building supplemental income streams that can support whatever retirement savings and plans you already have in place—if any.

Maybe you've been diligent and have a solid 401(k). Great. This will help you retire earlier or more comfortably.

Maybe you're starting late and your retirement savings are... well, let's just say "not where you'd like them to be." That's okay too. This will help you catch up.

Maybe you're somewhere in between—you've saved something, but you know it's not going to be enough to live the life you want. This book is especially for you.

The truth is, most of us fall into that last category. We've done what we could. We've contributed to our 401(k)s when we could afford to. We've tried to save. But life happened. Kids happened. Divorces happened. Medical bills happened. Job losses happened. The 2008 crash happened. The pandemic happened.

And now we're looking at retirement age on the horizon, and we're doing the math in our heads, and the numbers aren't adding up the way we hoped.

But here's the good news: You don't have to rely solely on what you've saved.

You can build income streams—starting today—that will supplement your retirement savings and give you the financial security and freedom you deserve.

That's what this book is about.

The Philosophy Behind the Cheat Codes

This book is built on one core belief: **You can create income that doesn't require you to trade hours for dollars.**

Most of us have spent our entire working lives in jobs where we get paid for our time. You show up, you work, you get paid. You don't show up, you don't get paid. It's a simple equation, but it's also a trap.

Because time is finite. You only have so many hours in a day, so many years in a career. And when you stop working—whether by choice or by force—the income stops too.

That's the old way. And it's not going to be enough.

The new way—the Genyus way—is to build income streams that work without you. Income that comes in whether you're working or not. Income that duplicates your effort, leverages your knowledge, and compounds over time.

This isn't about getting rich quick. It's not about crypto schemes or multi-level marketing or day trading. It's about building real, sustainable income streams using skills you already have and systems that are proven to work.

This book will show you how to:

· Identify skills and knowledge you already possess that can be monetized

· Build duplicative income streams that pay you repeatedly for work you do once

· Leverage your time and expertise so you're not always trading hours for dollars

· Plug the financial leaks that are draining your wealth right now

· Create a simple, clear plan that doesn't require a finance degree or a trust fund

These aren't theories. These are strategies that real people—people just like you—are using right now to build financial security for their future.

Who This Book Is For

This book is for Gen Xers who:

· Feel behind on retirement savings and want to catch up without panic or desperation

· Are tired of traditional financial advice that doesn't account for real life

· Want practical, actionable strategies they can start implementing today

· Are willing to put in some creative work now to help their future selves

· Don't trust the system to take care of them and want to build their own safety net

· Are skeptical of hype and want clear, jargon-free guidance

If that sounds like you, you're in the right place.

How to Use This Book

This book is organized into eight tracks—think of them as chapters, but also as individual strategies you can implement one at a time.

You don't have to read them in order. You don't have to implement all of them. You just need to pick the ones that resonate with you and take action.

Each track follows the same structure:

1. **Opening Story** – A relatable, real-world example that illustrates the concept

2. **The Old Way** – The outdated belief or system that's holding you back

3. **The Genyus Way** – The new mindset and approach that actually works

4. **Practical Examples** – Real strategies and methods you can use

5. **Why This Works** – The principles behind the strategy

6. **Reflection Prompts** – Questions to help you apply the concept to your life

7. **Actions You Can Take** – Specific, actionable steps you can start today

8. **Closing Thought** – A reminder to keep you motivated and focused

Here's how to get the most out of this book:

Read through all eight tracks first to get a sense of the full picture. Then, pick one or two strategies that feel most relevant to your situation and focus on those. Don't try to do everything at once. Pick one. Master it. Build momentum. Then add another.

This isn't a race. It's a process. And the best time to start is today.

A Word About Timing

I know what you might be thinking: "Is it too late? Should I have started this ten years ago?"

Maybe. But you didn't. And you can't change that. So the question isn't whether you should have started earlier—the question is: **What are you going to do now?**

Here's the truth: **It's not too late. But it is urgent.**

If you're in your forties, you have time to build significant supplemental income streams before retirement. If you're in your fifties, you have less time, but you can still make a massive impact. If you're in your sixties, you might be closer to retirement, but you can still create income streams that will support you for decades.

The key is to start. Not tomorrow. Not next month. Today.

Because every month you wait is a month of potential income you're leaving on the table. Every year you delay is a year of compounding growth you're missing out on.

You don't need to have it all figured out. You just need to start.

Pick one track. Read it. Take one action. Build from there.

The Latch-Key Generation Grows Up

We've always been good at figuring things out on our own. We had to be.

We came home to empty houses and made our own snacks. We figured out our homework without helicopter parents hovering over us. We navigated the world without GPS, without Google, without anyone holding our hand.

We learned to be resourceful. Self-reliant. Skeptical of authority. Comfortable with uncertainty.

And now, as we face retirement, we're going to need those skills again.

Because the system isn't going to save us. Social Security might be there, but it won't be enough. Pensions are gone. The company loyalty our parents believed in? It was a lie.

But that's okay. Because we've never really trusted the system anyway.

We've always known we'd have to take care of ourselves. And we've always been pretty damn good at it.

This book is just the next chapter in that story.

Let's Get Started

You picked up this book because you know something needs to change. You know that hoping for the best isn't a strategy. You know that you need to take action.

Good. That's the first step.

The second step is to keep reading. The third step is to pick one strategy and implement it. The fourth step is to keep going.

You don't need to be perfect. You don't need to have all the answers. You just need to start.

Because twenty years from now, you're going to look back at this moment—the moment you decided to take control of your financial future—and you're going to be grateful you did.

Your future self is counting on you.

Let's build something worth retiring to.

Disclaimer:

I am not a financial advisor, and nothing in this book should be construed as professional financial, investment, or legal advice. The strategies, examples, and recommendations presented here are based on my personal experiences, observations, and research—including methods I have used myself or witnessed others use successfully. Your results may vary based on your individual circumstances, risk tolerance, market conditions, and execution. Before implementing any financial strategy, especially those involving insurance products, investments, or tax implications, please consult with qualified professionals including financial advisors, tax professionals, and legal counsel who can evaluate your specific situation. No guarantees of success are implied or promised. You are solely responsible for your own financial decisions.

CHEAT CODE 1: Master This Before You Go Forward
Before you build anything, you need to believe you can.

1. Storytime

Summer, 1985. A public park somewhere in middle America. The smell of charcoal and lighter fluid mixing with the sweet smoke of burgers cooking over open flames. No smartphones. No tablets. No Wi-Fi. Just kids running around playing tag, adults standing in clusters with red Solo cups, and the distant sound of a boom box playing "Money for Nothing" by Dire Straits.

I was maybe ten years old, sitting at a picnic table with a stack of notebook paper covered in my drawings. I'd been working on something for weeks—a comic book about a man who could fly. Not just fly, but soar through the sky, saving people, fighting bad guys, being a hero. I was proud of it. Excited about it. I couldn't wait to show someone.

An uncle I didn't see very often walked over, beer in hand, and sat down across from me. He was making small talk, the way adults do when they're trying to be polite to kids they barely know.

"So, what have you been up to?" he asked, not really expecting much of an answer.

I lit up. "I've been working on my own comic book! It's about a man who can fly and—"

He chuckled. Not a mean chuckle, but the kind of chuckle that says, *Oh, you poor, naive kid.*

"That's already been done," he said, taking a sip of his beer. "Superman. He flies. Saves people. Been around since the '40s. You can't do that—it's already been done."

I felt my chest tighten. My excitement drained out of me like air from a punctured tire. I looked down at my drawings—my carefully sketched panels, my handwritten dialogue—and suddenly they looked stupid. Childish. Pointless.

I closed the notebook. I never showed anyone else. And I never finished that comic book.

That moment—that one dismissive comment from a well-meaning adult who thought he was teaching me to "think realistically"—killed something in me. Not permanently, but for a long time.

And here's the thing: **This story isn't unique to me. It happened to millions of Gen Xers.**

We grew up surrounded by small-minded people who shot down our dreams simply because they didn't possess the imagination or the vision to see what we saw. Teachers who told us to "be realistic." Parents who said, "That's nice, but you need a real job." Relatives who laughed at our ideas because they'd "already been done."

We were told that everything worth doing had already been done. That there was nothing new under the sun. That we were too late, too young, too inexperienced, too naive.

And a lot of us believed them.

But here's what that uncle at the BBQ didn't understand—and what a lot of people still don't understand: **Yes, Superman exists. But so does Batman, Spider-Man, Iron Man, Wonder Woman, the X-Men, and thousands of other heroes.**

Yes, there have been flying superheroes before. But there's never been *your* flying superhero. With *your* story. For *your* audience.

There's nothing new under the sun. But there are infinite ways to share something in a new light.

And that's what this track is about.

Before you build any income stream, before you create any product, before you launch any side hustle—you need to master this mindset. Because if you don't, you'll quit before you even start. You'll talk yourself out of it. You'll let the voices—external and internal—convince you that it's already been done, that you're too late, that someone else is already doing it better.

And you'll miss your shot.

So let's fix that. Right now.

2. The Old Way

The old way says: **"It's already been done. Why bother?"**

Someone's already written a book about retirement. Someone's already created a course on investing. Someone's already started a podcast about personal finance. Someone's already selling the thing you want to sell, teaching the thing you want to teach, building the thing you want to build.

So why bother?

The old way says: **"You need a completely original idea."**

You need to invent something no one's ever seen before. You need to be the first. You need to be revolutionary. You need to be Elon Musk or Steve Jobs or some genius disruptor who changes the world.

And since you're not that, you might as well not even try.

The old way says: **"If it's been done, there's no room for you."**

The market is saturated. The competition is too fierce. The big players have already won. You're too late. You missed the boat. You should have started ten years ago.

This is the voice that keeps most people from ever starting.

It's the voice of that uncle at the BBQ. It's the voice of every teacher who told you to be realistic. It's the voice of every well-meaning friend who said, "That's a nice idea, but..."

And it's the voice inside your own head that whispers, *Who do you think you are? You're not special. You're not an expert. You don't have anything new to say.*

That voice is a liar.

And if you listen to it, you'll never build anything.

3. The Genyus Way

"There's nothing new under the sun. But there are infinite ways to share something in a new light."

Here's the truth: **Yes, it's been done. And that's exactly why you should do it.**

The fact that something has been done before proves there's a market for it. It proves people want it. It proves it works.

Your job isn't to invent something completely new. Your job is to **do it for your people, in your voice, with your perspective.**

Think about this book. There are thousands of books about retirement. Hundreds about building income streams. Dozens about financial independence.

> **But there's only one written specifically for Gen Xers who are skeptical, self-reliant, and tired of being told what they should have done twenty years ago.**

That's the difference.

Superman exists. But Spider-Man exists too. And they both fly (or swing). And they're both massively successful. Because they speak to different people in different ways.

The Genyus way understands four critical rules:

Rule 1: Don't let other people's lack of vision influence you.

This includes the negative voices inside your own head. When someone says, "That's already been done," what they're really saying is, "I don't have the imagination to see how you could do it differently." That's their limitation, not yours. Don't let their small thinking shrink your vision.

Rule 2: Choose a persona type that thousands of people identify with proudly.

Don't try to speak to everyone. Speak to someone specific. Gen Xers. Fathers. Grandparents. Teachers. Basketball fans. Dog lovers. People who grew up in the '80s. People who hate corporate jobs. People who feel behind on retirement. The more specific your audience, the more powerfully you can speak to them—and the more they'll feel like you're talking directly to them.

Rule 3: Be sure your title (or offer) speaks to a common pain point or problem this group experiences.

"The Gen X Cheat Codes for Retirement Income" works because it speaks directly to a pain point: Gen Xers who feel behind on retirement and want practical solutions. It's not "Retirement Planning for Everyone." It's not "Financial Freedom in 10 Easy Steps." It's specific. It's targeted. It promises to solve a real problem for a real group of people.

Rule 4: Deliver on your promise to offer real solutions.

Don't just identify the problem—solve it. Give people actionable steps. Give them strategies they can implement. Give them hope and a path forward. If you promise cheat codes, deliver cheat codes. If you promise solutions, deliver solutions. Your credibility is built on whether you actually help people or just talk about helping them.

These four rules are the foundation of everything you'll build.

Master them, and you can create income streams that matter. Ignore them, and you'll either never start or you'll create something nobody wants.

4. Practical Examples: How This Works in Real Life

Let's look at how this plays out across different income streams and ideas.

Example 1: The Retirement Book That Already Exists

There are thousands of retirement books. But "The Gen X Cheat Codes for Retirement Income" is different because it speaks to a specific persona (Gen X), addresses a specific pain point (feeling behind on retirement), and delivers in a specific voice (skeptical, self-reliant, no-BS). It's not trying to be everything to everyone. It's trying to be exactly what one group of people needs. That specificity is what makes it work.

Example 2: The Fitness Coach Who Targets Busy Dads

There are millions of fitness coaches. But a coach who specifically targets "busy dads over 40 who want to lose the gut without spending hours in the gym" is speaking to a persona (busy dads), a pain point (no time, aging body), and a promise (results without endless gym time). That's not a new idea—it's an old idea done for a specific audience in a specific way.

Example 3: The Meal Prep Service for Teachers

Meal prep services exist everywhere. But a service that specifically targets teachers—"Healthy Meal Prep for Teachers Who Don't Have Time to Cook During the School Year"—speaks directly to a persona (teachers), a pain point (no time during the school year), and a solution (pre-made, healthy meals). Teachers will see that and think, *That's for me.* Generic meal prep services won't get that same response.

Example 4: The Budgeting Course for Single Moms

Budgeting courses are everywhere. But "The Single Mom's Guide to Budgeting on One Income" speaks to a specific persona (single moms), a specific pain point (managing money on one income), and a specific promise (practical budgeting strategies). It's not revolutionary. It's targeted.

Example 5: The Productivity System for Creative Freelancers

Productivity systems are a dime a dozen. But "The Creative Freelancer's Anti-Burnout Productivity System" speaks to a persona (creative freelancers), a pain point (burnout and inconsistent income), and a promise (productivity without burning out). It's the same productivity principles everyone teaches—but packaged for a specific audience who will feel seen and understood.

See the pattern?

It's not about inventing something new. It's about taking something that works and making it specific, targeted, and relevant to a group of people who will see themselves in it.

That's how you cut through the noise. That's how you build something people actually want.

5. Why This Works

This approach works because of four powerful psychological principles:

It creates instant connection. When someone sees a title or offer that speaks directly to them—"Gen X," "Busy Dads," "Single Moms," "Teachers"—they immediately feel seen. They think, *This is for me.* That connection is instant and powerful. Generic offers don't create that feeling.

It eliminates competition. When you're specific, you're not competing with everyone. You're competing with the handful of people who are also speaking to your specific audience. And if you do it well, you're not competing at all—you're the obvious choice.

It builds trust faster. When you speak directly to someone's pain point and demonstrate that you understand their specific situation, they trust you faster. They believe you can help them because you clearly understand them.

It makes marketing easier. When you know exactly who you're talking to, you know where to find them, what to say to them, and how to reach them. Marketing a "retirement book" is nearly impossible. Marketing "The Gen X Cheat Codes for Retirement Income" is simple—go where Gen Xers hang out and speak their language.

This is how quiet millionaires think. They don't try to be every-thing to everyone. They pick a lane. They get specific. They speak to a real person with a real problem. And they deliver real solutions.

6. Reflection Prompts

Before you move forward, answer these questions honestly. Write them down.

What idea have you talked yourself out of because "it's al-ready been done"? Be honest. What have you wanted to create, build, or start—but didn't because you thought someone else was already doing it? Write it down. Because that idea might still be worth pursuing if you apply the four rules.

What persona type do you belong to that you're proud of? Are you a Gen Xer? A parent? A teacher? A veteran? A small business owner? A creative? What group do you identify with strongly? Because that's likely a group you can speak to authentically.

What pain point or problem does that group experience that you've also experienced? What do they struggle with? What keeps them up at night? What have you figured out that they're still trying to solve? That's your opening. That's your angle.

7. Actions You Can Take

Don't just read this and move on. Take action today.

Action Step: The Four-Rule Filter

Before you build any income stream, run it through the four-rule filter:

Rule 1 Check: Am I letting someone else's lack of vision stop me? Am I listening to the voices that say "it's already been done" instead of asking "how can I do this for my people?" If you're stuck because of other people's opinions (or your own negative self-talk), write down those objections. Then cross them out. They're not facts—they're fears.

Rule 2 Check: Have I chosen a specific persona type? Who exactly am I speaking to? "Everyone" is not an answer. Get specific. Write down the persona: Gen Xers, busy moms, teachers, freelancers, retirees, dog owners, etc. If you can't name your audience in two or three words, you're not specific enough.

Rule 3 Check: Does my title or offer speak to a common pain point this group experiences? What problem are you solving? What pain are you addressing? If your offer doesn't immediately make your target audience think, *That's exactly what I need,* go back and refine it.

Rule 4 Check: Can I actually deliver real solutions? Do you have the knowledge, experience, or ability to help this group solve their problem? If not, can you learn it, partner with someone, or position yourself as a guide who's one step ahead? Don't promise what you can't deliver—but don't underestimate what you already know.

Here are some other specific actions you can take right now:

Pick one idea you've been sitting on and run it through the four-rule filter. Does it pass? If not, how can you adjust it so it does?

Write down three persona types you could authentically speak to. Which one feels most natural? Which one has a pain point you've personally solved or are currently solving?

Go to Amazon or Google and search for products, books, or courses in your area of interest. Notice how the successful ones are targeted and specific. Study their titles. Study their descriptions. Learn from what's working.

Stop saying "it's already been done" and start asking "how can I do this for my people in my voice?"

Create a working title for your idea using this formula: [Persona Type] + [Pain Point/Problem] + [Promise/Solution]. Example: "The Busy Dad's Guide to Getting Fit Without Living in the Gym."

8. Closing Thought

"There's nothing new under the sun. But there are infinite ways to share something in a new light."

That uncle at the BBQ was wrong. Yes, Superman existed. But that didn't mean my flying superhero couldn't exist too. It just meant I needed to figure out what made mine different. What made mine matter. Who it was for.

I didn't know that then. I was just a kid with a notebook full of drawings and a dream that got crushed by someone who couldn't see past what already existed.

But I know it now. And you need to know it too.

Because the world doesn't need another generic solution. It needs your specific solution for your specific people.

There are thousands of retirement books. But there's only one for Gen Xers who are skeptical, self-reliant, and tired of being lectured about what they should have done differently.

There are millions of fitness coaches. But there's only one who speaks specifically to busy dads over 40 who want results without living in the gym.

There are countless meal prep services. But there's only one designed specifically for teachers who don't have time to cook during the school year.

Your job isn't to invent something completely new. Your job is to take something that works and make it yours.

Pick your people. Speak to their pain. Deliver real solutions. And ignore everyone who says, "That's already been done."

Because yes, it has been done. And that's exactly why you should do it—for your people, in your voice, in your way.

The world is full of people who need exactly what you have to offer. But they'll never find you if you're trying to speak to everyone.

Get specific. Get targeted. Get clear.

Master these four rules before you go forward, and everything else in this book will work.

Ignore them, and you'll build something nobody wants—or worse, you'll never build anything at all.

So let's make a deal right now:

You will not let other people's lack of vision stop you. You will choose your people. You will speak to their pain. And you will deliver real solutions.

That's the foundation. Now let's build something worth retiring to.

CHEAT CODE 2: The Art of Self-Duplication

Do the work once, get paid many times.

1. Storytime

When I finally got my first job after receiving my degree, I thought I was on my way to the big money. I didn't know how I was going to get there, but I had been convinced through television shows, movies, and the advice of adults I trusted my entire life that this was the path to financial freedom: get an education, get a job in a corporation, work your way up by showing how smart and resourceful you are, watch that money build over time until you finally retire and relish all the good decisions you made.

The reality was much different.

I had a job, my own cubicle in the midst of hundreds of others. I was an accounts payable processor; paying company bills that never ended. It didn't take me long to realize that the path I had envisioned towards success was probably not going to unfold the way I'd planned. My paychecks were just enough to cover the bills, and the thought of putting away money for savings was almost a joke.

I'll never forget the day I paused and looked up over the piles of unprocessed invoices I still had to pay. I saw a group of men walking into a meeting room. They were all dressed pretty much the same. Khaki pants, loafers, polo shirts tucked in. All of them had the same "I'm glad I have this job" grin. I knew each of them lived pretty much the same life. Two or three kids, two cars, a house, in-laws, and senior C-level executives and vice presidents in cushy jobs above them that were not leaving any time soon, so there weren't many opportunities to go up.

There was no up; just where you were at.

I wondered in despair, "Am I looking at my future?"

A few years later I was able to put a couple of skills into my pocket: graphic design, copywriting, and web development. Those skills combined formed my own financial "Voltron." I was creating websites for small businesses who were happy to hand me a check for the work I did. I was ecstatic. In my mind I was finally moving away from the chains of corporate glass ceiling life. In my head I had a "business."

There was only one problem.

I liked cashing checks for website work; but in order for me to get another check, I had to trade my time for the money. It was just another form of the corporate trap I thought I'd escaped. I thought I owned a business, but what I actually owned was a job. Nothing wrong with that, by the way. But it was still no guarantee of freedom or retirement facilitation.

It wasn't until I was 33 and reading a LOT of books about wealth when it finally hit me. I needed to duplicate myself if I was ever going to obtain wealth. I needed to find a way to do work once, but get paid multiple times for that same work. The only problem was "how."

I had read Robert Kiyosaki's book *Rich Dad, Poor Dad*, I'd read Tim Ferriss' *The 4-Hour Work Week*, and they were getting me closer to my solution, but it was still elusive.

And then it hit me.

I may not have money to buy a franchise, or invest in real estate, but I did know how to build websites, and websites had addresses, just like real estate. It was then I cracked the code: I would stop building websites for one-time checks. Instead, I would build websites for myself and treat them like properties; leasing them to small businesses once they were ranked on Google and capturing sales leads from customers.

I had done it. I'd taken what I knew how to do, and turned it into my duplication escape plan.

Within eighteen months, I had built twelve websites generating passive lead flow. I wasn't trading hours anymore—I was collecting rent on digital real estate I owned. The work I did once kept paying me month after month. That shift—from trading time for money to building assets that worked while I slept—changed everything.

That's the art of self-duplication. And once you see it, you can't unsee it.

2. The Old Way

Most of us were raised on a simple formula:

"Work hard, get paid, repeat."

It sounded honest—and it was—but nobody told us the downside: hard work that doesn't multiply can never set you free.

The old way looks like this:

· Trade hours for dollars.

· If you want more money, work more hours.

· Loyalty and effort will eventually buy you security.

· Keep your head down, stay busy, and hope for a promotion.

That's what we were told. And for a lot of people, it worked—sort of. You could survive. Pay bills. Maybe take a vacation once a year.

But here's the problem: **effort and loyalty can't scale.**

Your income has a ceiling the size of your energy. The day you get sick, burned out, or just tired of the grind, the income stops. You're always one layoff, one health crisis, or one bad quarter away from financial panic.

The old way keeps you running, but it never sets you free.

3. The Genyus Way

"Do the work once, but design it to pay you again and again."

That's self-duplication—the single biggest wealth leap a person can make.

Think of it like cloning your best work. You perform once, and that performance keeps earning because it can be watched, read, used, or taught again.

Self-duplication isn't about building an empire overnight. It's about training your mind to ask one powerful question every day:

"How can I make this hour pay me more than once?"

Quiet millionaires live by this principle. They don't just work harder—they work smarter by building systems, products, or structures that keep working even when they aren't.

This isn't luck or tech magic; it's math and mindset. It's learning to stop renting out your time and start owning the results of your time.

Here's what that looks like in practice:

· Instead of trading an hour for a paycheck, you create something once that earns repeatedly.

· Instead of starting from zero every Monday, you wake up to income you didn't have to trade time for.

· Instead of being stuck in the labor economy, you enter the asset economy.

You stop being an employee of your time and become the owner of your results.

4. Practical Examples

Type: Creative

Example: Write a short eBook or workbook once.

How It Duplicates: Sell it forever on Amazon, Gumroad, or your own site.

Type: Service-Based

Example: Train someone else to do part of your process.

How It Duplicates: Every task you delegate frees you to earn again elsewhere.

Type: Product-Based

Example: Create art, then sell digital prints.

How It Duplicates: One painting, infinite prints through print-on-demand.

Type: Knowledge-Based

Example: Teach your skill through a video, course, or guide.

How It Duplicates: One lesson, hundreds of students over time.

Type: Lifestyle-Based

Example: Love animals? Offer in-home pet-sitting while you work from home.

How It Duplicates: One hour, two incomes—your remote job plus pet care fees.

Type: Digital Real Estate

Example: Build niche websites that rank on Google and lease them to local businesses.

How It Duplicates: One build, recurring monthly lease payments.

Remember: The goal isn't perfection; it's pattern recognition. Once your brain starts spotting duplication opportunities, it never stops.

5. Why This Works

Self-duplication moves you from the **labor economy** to the **asset economy**.

In the labor economy, you get paid once for every hour you work. Your income resets to zero every week. You're always starting over.

In the asset economy, you get paid repeatedly for work you did once. Your income compounds. You build momentum instead of just surviving.

Every duplicated asset is like planting a tree: it starts small, but it keeps producing shade and fruit year after year. Five trees? That's breathing room. Ten trees? That's freedom. Fifty trees? That's legacy.

Here's the math that changes everything:

One hour of work = one paycheck = you stay broke.
One hour of duplication = infinite paychecks = you build wealth.

Quiet millionaires understand this deeply. They don't chase hours—they chase architecture. They don't just work—they build systems that work for them.

And the beautiful part? You don't need a trust fund, a fancy degree, or a lucky break to start. You just need to shift how you think about your time and your talents.

6. Reflection Prompts

Take a moment and ask yourself these questions. Write down your answers—don't just think them.

·   **What's one task or talent you repeat often that could be turned into a product, guide, or system?**

·   **If you had to earn money this month without working extra hours, what could you package or teach?**

·   **What stops you from creating once and releasing it—fear, perfectionism, or lack of time? Write it down and question it.**

These aren't rhetorical questions. They're the beginning of your duplication strategy.

7. Actions You Can Take

Don't just read this and move on. Take one small step today.

Action Step: Build Your "1-Hour Clone"

Pick one idea—something you know how to do well—and spend one focused hour creating or documenting something that could earn twice.

Here are some examples to get you started:

· Record a 10-minute tutorial on something people always ask you about.

· Write a simple checklist or template and sell it for $5 on Etsy or Gumroad.

· Take one piece of your work (art, writing, design) and turn it into a digital product.

· Document a process you do at work and offer to teach it as a mini-course.

· Build one simple website around a local service niche and test ranking it on Google.

Upload it. Share it. Teach it. Sell it.

Don't worry about scale—your only goal is to prove duplication works.

Once you feel that first duplicated dollar come in, the game changes forever. Because now you know: **you can do work once and get paid many times.**

That knowledge is worth more than any degree.

8. Closing Thought

"Hard work builds income. Smart duplication builds freedom."

You've spent years working hard. Now it's time to work smart. The art of self-duplication isn't about doing more—it's about designing your effort to pay you long after the work is done.

One hour. Many returns. That's how freedom compounds.

CHEAT CODE 3: Your Hidden Leverage

You're sitting on something valuable—you just stopped seeing it.

1. Storytime

Her name was Maria, and when we first talked, she was convinced she had nothing to offer.

"I'm just a medical assistant," she told me, her voice flat with resignation. "I go to work, I come home, I crash on the couch. That's it. That's my life."

Maria had been working at the same clinic for seven years. She was good at her job—patients loved her, doctors trusted her—but she never felt like she was getting ahead. Her paycheck covered the bills, barely, and the idea of saving money felt like a cruel joke.

"I don't have a degree," she said. "So I can't get a better job. And I definitely can't start some side business or whatever. I don't have any skills."

I asked her what she knew how to do.

"Nothing," she said quickly. "I can't draw. I can't play an instrument. I can't sing or code or do any of that stuff people make money from online. I'm not special."

I could hear the weight in her words. She'd convinced herself that because she didn't fit into the narrow boxes society calls "talented," she had nothing of value to offer the world.

So I changed the question.

"What do you like to do?"

She paused. "I don't know. I guess... on the weekends, when I can spare a couple of dollars, I like spending time with my friends."

"What do you do with them?"

"We go out to eat, mostly. Try new places. Coffee shops, dessert spots, little hole-in-the-wall restaurants. I'm kind of a foodie, I guess. I know all the good local spots."

I smiled. "Then you do have a hidden talent."

She looked confused.

"You know exactly how to help people eat like a local," I said. "Tourists are always looking for that. So are people who just moved to town. So are couples looking for new date night ideas. You have knowledge people would pay for—you just didn't realize it was valuable."

Maria sat with that for a moment. I could see the gears turning.

"So... what do I do with it?"

"Start small," I told her. "Make a list of your favorite spots. Your go-to coffee shop, the best tacos, the dessert place you always recommend. Write it down. Then sell it for five bucks."

She laughed. "Who's going to pay five dollars for a list?"

"Try it and see."

A week later, she posted casually on social media: "I put together a list of my favorite local spots to eat, grab coffee, and get dessert. $5 if you want it."

Within two days, she'd sold twelve copies.

Some people had family coming into town and wanted fresh ideas. Others were tired of the same date night restaurants. A few were new to the city and didn't know where to start.

Maria was shocked. "People actually paid me for this?"

"That's your hidden leverage," I said. "What's obvious to you is magic to someone else."

Over the next few months, Maria expanded. She created themed lists: best brunch spots, pet-friendly patios, late-night eats, romantic date ideas, budget-friendly meals under $15. She started a simple Instagram page where she posted photos and short reviews. She began getting messages from local businesses asking if she'd feature them.

Within a year, Maria had turned her weekend hobby into a steady side income. She wasn't rich, but she wasn't stuck anymore either. She had breathing room. She had options. And most importantly, she had proof that she wasn't "just" anything.

She had value the whole time—she just needed someone to help her see it.

That's the power of hidden leverage. It's not about being special. It's about recognizing that what you do naturally, what you know deeply, what people already ask you about—that's your starting point.

You don't need to invent something new. You just need to name what you already do well, and then let the world pay you for it.

2. The Old Way

Most people think leverage means money, connections, or degrees. They look at their lives and think:

"I'm just good at my job."
"Everyone already knows this stuff."
"I'm not expert enough to charge for it."

That's the old way of thinking. It keeps you small because you confuse effort with value. You think something only has worth if it feels hard or official.

The old way looks like this:

· Dismiss your own knowledge because it comes easily to you.

· Assume that if you can do it, everyone can.

· Wait for permission—a degree, a certification, a title—before you believe you're "qualified."

· Overlook the questions people keep asking you because you think they're just being polite.

Meanwhile, people are Googling the very thing that comes naturally to you. They're paying strangers on the internet to teach them
what you already know.

The old way keeps you invisible—not because you lack value, but
because you've trained yourself not to see it.

3. The Genyus Way

"If people keep asking, that's proof of demand."
"What's obvious to you is magic to someone else."

This is your hidden leverage—the ability to turn ordinary knowledge into income, influence, or freedom using today's tools.

You don't need to invent something new. You don't need a business degree or a massive following. You just need to:

· **Name** what you already do well.

· **Claim** it as valuable.

· **Monetize** it using simple, modern tools.

Quiet millionaires understand this deeply. They notice what the
world keeps asking of them, and they turn those requests into
repeatable systems, lessons, or products.

Here's the shift:

Old belief: "I'm not special."

New truth: "I have proof of value—people already ask for my help."

Old belief: "I'm too late to start."

New truth: "The internet never sleeps; there's always room for one more voice done well."

Old belief: "I need a big following."

New truth: "I just need one clear offer that solves one clear problem."

Your hidden leverage isn't out there somewhere. It's the thing everyone keeps thanking you for—you just haven't charged for it yet.

4. Practical Examples

Source of Skill: Work Skill (Excel, project management, sales)

Hidden Leverage: Create short tutorials or templates.

Modern Tool to Monetize It: YouTube, Gumroad, Canva, Fiverr

Source of Skill: Hobby (gardening, home repair, cooking)

Hidden Leverage: Teach it or make digital cheat sheets.

Modern Tool to Monetize It: TikTok/Instagram Reels, Substack, Etsy

Source of Skill: Life Experience (divorce recovery, single parenting, career changes)

Hidden Leverage: Write micro-guides or record support audios.

Modern Tool to Monetize It: Amazon KDP, Notion templates, online workshops

Source of Skill: Local Knowledge (best restaurants, hidden gems, date night spots)

Hidden Leverage: Curate lists or create city guides.

Modern Tool to Monetize It: Instagram, Gumroad, Payhip, Etsy

Source of Skill: Organizational Talent (meal planning, budgeting, decluttering)

Hidden Leverage: Sell templates, checklists, or mini-courses.

Modern Tool to Monetize It: Notion, Canva, Teachable, Gumroad

Source of Skill: Creative Eye (interior design, photography, styling)

Hidden Leverage: Offer virtual consultations or sell presets/templates.

Modern Tool to Monetize It: Zoom, Calendly, Lightroom presets, Etsy

Notice: none of these are exotic. They're everyday skills translated into value with modern leverage—automation, publishing, and reach.

5. Why This Works

You already spent years learning, failing, and refining—that effort is stored value.

Technology is simply the multiplier.

When you publish a guide, teach a lesson, or automate a process, you let that stored value keep paying you back. That's real leverage: knowledge that works while you sleep.

Here's why hidden leverage is so powerful:

· **It costs nothing to start.** You already have the knowledge. You just need to package it.

· **It meets existing demand.** If people keep asking, the market is already there.

· **It compounds over time.** One guide sold today can sell again tomorrow, next month, next year.

· **It builds confidence.** Every sale proves you have value. That belief changes everything.

Quiet millionaires aren't better than you—they're just brave enough to believe their experience counts. They see the questions people ask them as clues, not compliments. And they act on those clues.

You can too.

6. Reflection Prompts

Take a moment and answer these questions honestly. Write them down—don't just think about them.

· **What's something people have asked you for help with more than once?**

· **What problem do you solve so naturally that you barely notice it anymore?**

· **If you had to teach one thing for free all day long, what would keep your energy high?**

Your answers are your roadmap. They're pointing you toward your hidden leverage.

7. Actions You Can Take

Don't just read this and move on. Take action today.

Action Step: The Three-Question Inventory

Grab a piece of paper or open a notes app. Answer these three questions:

1. **What have three different people asked me for help with in the last year?**

2. **What do I know how to do that most people struggle with?**

3. **What do I do in my free time that people say they wish they could do?**

Write down everything that comes to mind. Don't filter. Don't judge. Just list.

Now circle the one that feels easiest or most energizing. That's your first piece of hidden leverage.

Next, ask yourself: **"How can I share or sell this in a way that keeps paying me?"**

Here are some simple starting points:

· Create a $5 guide or checklist and sell it on Gumroad or Etsy.

· Record a 10-minute tutorial and post it on YouTube or TikTok.

· Write a short how-to post and share it on social media with a link to "buy the full version."

· Offer a 30-minute consultation on Zoom for $25–$50.

· Build a simple email list and share one tip per week, with a paid product at the end.

Pick one. Do it this week. Don't wait for perfect—just start.

That first sale will change how you see yourself forever.

8. Closing Thought

"Your leverage isn't out there somewhere. It's the thing everyone keeps thanking you for—you just haven't charged for it yet."

You don't need to be an expert. You don't need a platform. You don't need permission.

You just need to name what you already know, claim it as valuable, and let the world pay you for it.

That's your hidden leverage. And it's been waiting for you all along.

CHEAT CODE 4: The $100 Test

How you treat $100 reveals your money operating system.

1. Opening Story

I grew up poor in the 80s. Thankfully, the economy back then wasn't anywhere near where it is today. If your grandmother sent you $10 for your birthday, that money could stretch a bit if you rationed the Twinkies, Hostess Apple Pies, and ice cream truck visits just right.

But I found that there were two types of kids when it came to money.

There were those that were consistently poor, so being able to spend money was a means to feel like the other kids, even if just for a little while. When you got that $10, you spent it fast—because who knew when you'd get another $10? You wanted to feel normal, even if it only lasted a weekend.

And then there were the kids that saved the money. They were often able to save because their parents were able to give them the type of life where they didn't go without very often, so saving wasn't a problem. These were also the kids that always had the best stuff, like the full He-Man Castle Grayskull playset, or the entire Strawberry Shortcake line of dolls. Very annoying to the rest of us.

But living in these two worlds did something else; they solidified a mindset towards money that often goes on to inform our decision making as we moved into the 90s, 2000s, and beyond.

I was the first type of kid. Every dollar I got burned a hole in my pocket. It wasn't that I was irresponsible—I just didn't know any other way to think about money except as something that disappeared. Money came, money went. That was the cycle.

Fast forward to my twenties. I had a job, a paycheck, and a little bit of breathing room for the first time in my life. And you know what I did? I spent it. Not recklessly—just... constantly. A night out here, a new gadget there, takeout instead of cooking, clothes I didn't really need. Nothing felt like a big deal because each purchase was small.

But the pattern was the same as when I was a kid: **money in, money out.**

It wasn't until I was in my early thirties that I realized something: **I was still operating with the same money mindset I had when I was eight years old.**

I remember the moment it clicked. I got a $500 bonus at work—unexpected, exciting. My first thought was, "Finally, I can get that new TV I've been wanting."

But then I paused. I'd been reading about investing, about building wealth, about how rich people think differently. And I asked myself a question I'd never asked before:

"What would the wealthy version of me do with this money?"

The answer wasn't "buy a TV."

The wealthy version of me would ask: "How can this money work for me instead of just disappearing?"

So I did something I'd never done before. I took that $500 and opened a Roth IRA. I put the whole thing in an index fund and didn't touch it.

It felt weird. It felt like I was denying myself something I "deserved." But a few months later, I checked the account. That $500 had grown to $540. I hadn't done anything—it just grew.

That's when I understood: **every dollar is a choice between disappearing or duplicating.**

And the way you treat $100 today reveals which path you're on.

2. The Old Way

Most of us were taught that money has one purpose:

"Money is for spending."
"I earned it, I deserve to enjoy it."

Nothing wrong with that. You should enjoy your life. But most people only know one use for money: subtraction.

The old way looks like this:

· Every dollar you get immediately starts disappearing—spent, swiped, or scrolled away.

· You think of money as temporary, not trustworthy.

· Small purchases don't feel like a big deal, so you make them constantly.

· When extra money comes in—a bonus, a tax refund, a gift—you treat it like "fun money" and spend it fast.

· You never pause to ask, "Could this do more for me?"

That pattern teaches your brain that money is something that leaves, not something that stays and grows.

It keeps you in survival mode, even when you earn more. Because no matter how much comes in, it all goes out just as fast.

3. The Genyus Way

"Money is a tool for building."
"Every dollar is an employee—give it a job."

Quiet millionaires don't hoard money—they deploy it. When they get $100, they ask:

· **"How can this make more?"**

· **"What small asset could I buy?"**

· **"What skill could I invest in?"**

· **"What system could I improve?"**

They think like builders, not spenders. They don't see dollars as fuel for consumption—they see them as seeds that can grow new trees.

They're not stingy. They simply understand multiplication.

When you multiply money, it doesn't just make you richer—it makes you calmer. Because now, your money works for you, not against you.

Here's the shift:

Old belief: "I should enjoy my money now."
New truth: "I can enjoy my money *and* make it work for me."

Old belief: "Small amounts don't matter."
New truth: "Small amounts repeated build empires."

Old belief: "I'll invest when I have more."
New truth: "If I can multiply $100, I can multiply anything."

The $100 Test isn't about deprivation—it's about awareness. Every transaction teaches your subconscious what you believe about money:

"I consume it" or **"I command it."**

4. Practical Examples

You get a $100 bonus.

Old Way: Buy something you've been eyeing.
Genyus Way: Buy a course or tool that teaches a new income skill.

You sell something on Marketplace.

Old Way: Treat it like free cash, order dinner.
Genyus Way: Buy a course or tool that teaches a new income skill.

You get a tax refund.

Old Way: Vacation or shopping spree.
Genyus Way: Divide it: 50% invest, 25% skill-upgrade, 25% enjoy intentionally.

You receive a gift card.

Old Way: Burn it fast on impulse buys.
Genyus Way: Use it to purchase supplies for a creative idea or side project.

You find $20 in an old jacket.

Old Way: "Free money!"—spend it immediately.
Genyus Way: Add it to your investment account or emergency fund.

You get paid for a side gig.

Old Way: Treat yourself—you earned it.
Genyus Way: Reinvest 70% into growing that side gig; enjoy 30%.

This isn't about guilt—it's about awareness. Every transaction teaches your subconscious what you believe about money.

5. Why This Works

Your brain builds patterns from repetition. Every time you pause before spending, you teach your mind that you're in charge of money, not the other way around.

When that becomes automatic, you start finding leverage everywhere—not just with dollars, but with time, energy, and opportunity.

Here's why the $100 Test is so powerful:

· **It reveals your money operating system.** How you treat small money predicts how you'll treat big money.

· **It builds the multiplication habit.** Once you see $100 grow, you start asking "what else can grow?"

· **It creates calm.** When money works for you, you stop living paycheck to paycheck—even if your paycheck stays the same.

· **It compounds confidence.** Every smart choice proves you're capable of wealth, not just survival.

Quiet millionaires master this early because they understand:

"If I can multiply $100, I can multiply $1,000—and eventually, anything."

The amount doesn't matter. The pattern does. Build the reflex now, and it'll multiply forever.

6. Reflection Prompts

Take a moment and answer these questions honestly. Write them down—don't just think about them.

· **Think back to the last unexpected $100 you got. What did you do with it?**

· **How often do you ask, "What can this create?" before spending?**

· **What small asset, tool, or upgrade could $100 buy that would make life easier or income steadier?**

Your answers will show you which operating system is running: consumption or multiplication.

7. Actions You Can Take

Don't just read this and move on. Take action today.

Action Step: The Next $100 Rule

The next time you receive unexpected money—a bonus, refund, gift, side gig payment, or even finding cash in an old coat—pause before you spend it.

Ask yourself these three questions:

1. **Can this buy me time?** (Housecleaner, meal prep, VA—anything that frees you to build.)

2. **Can this buy me leverage?** (Tools, software, education that multiplies your output.)

3. **Can this buy me peace?** (Health, therapy, environments that reduce stress.)

If the answer to any of these is yes, do that instead of spending it on something that just feels good in the moment.

Here are some specific examples:

· Put $100 into a Roth IRA or index fund.

· Buy a book or course that teaches a skill you can monetize.

· Invest in tools or supplies for a duplication project (Track 1).

· Pay down $100 of high-interest debt (Track 8).

· Add it to your emergency fund in a high-yield savings account.

· Use it to test a small ad for your side business.

Pick one. Do it this week.

Then watch what happens. That $100 will teach you more about wealth than any seminar ever could.

8. Closing Thought

"Every dollar you spend disappears. Every dollar you deploy becomes a teammate. The question is—who's really on your payroll?"

You don't need more money to start building wealth. You just need to change what you do with the money you already have.

The $100 Test isn't about the amount—it's about the pattern. Master the pattern with small money, and big money will follow.

Start today. Your future self is watching.

CHEAT CODE 5: The Economy of Attention
Your focus is your fortune.

1. Opening Story

Gen Xers are uniquely qualified to understand just how important time is. We grew up in an era where things like microwaves and commercial-free programming didn't exist. If you wanted food heated up, you had to get the stovetop or the oven warm. If you wanted to watch your favorite show, you had to be patient and endure the commercials.

Even communicating with the people we loved was time sensitive. We couldn't just reach into our pockets and call someone. We waited until we got home; or if it was an emergency, we stopped by a payphone, checked the change return for any leftover change, dropped in our coins and hoped they were by the phone.

Those of us from Generation X deeply understand how important attention can be.

We remember what it was like to wait. To focus. To commit to one thing at a time because we had no choice. When your favorite song came on the radio, you stopped everything and hit "record" on your cassette player. When your show was on, you sat down and watched it—no pause button, no rewind. You were either present or you missed it.

But somewhere along the way, we lost that skill.

The world changed. Technology gave us instant everything—instant communication, instant entertainment, instant answers. And at first, it felt like freedom. No more waiting. No more missing out.

But what we didn't realize was that we were trading one kind of freedom for another. We gained convenience, but we lost something far more valuable: our ability to focus.

I remember the moment I realized how much my attention had been hijacked. I was sitting at my desk, trying to write. I had an hour of free time—a rare gift—and I was determined to use it well. But within ten minutes, I'd checked my email twice, scrolled through social media, read three news headlines, and responded to a text. By the time I looked up, thirty minutes were gone. I hadn't written a single word.

I felt frustrated, but not surprised. This had become normal.

That's when it hit me: **I wasn't in control of my attention anymore. My attention was being spent—no, stolen—OK, the truth is I was giving it away to a thousand tiny distractions I'd invited into my life.**

And if attention is the currency that buys focus, and focus is what creates value, then I was broke. Not financially—but mentally. I was spending my most valuable resource on things that gave me nothing in return.

Quiet millionaires understand something most people don't: **attention is your first currency.** Before you can earn money, build wealth, or create anything of value, you have to protect your attention. Because where your attention goes, your energy follows. And where your energy goes, your results follow.

If you're constantly distracted, you'll never build anything that lasts. Not because you're not smart enough or hardworking enough—but because you're spending your attention budget on noise instead of signal.

The good news? Gen Xers already know how to do this. We just forgot. We grew up in a world that demanded focus. Now we just need to remember how to demand it from ourselves.

2. The Old Way

Most of us were taught that productivity means staying busy:

"Stay busy. Always be doing something."
"If I'm multitasking, I'm productive."

That's the noise we grew up with. We were taught that activity equals progress. The more you're doing, the better you're doing.

But busyness is often just distraction with a timecard. When everything gets your attention, nothing grows.

The old way looks like this: You wake up and immediately grab your phone. You scroll through social media while your coffee brews. You check email during breakfast. You listen to a podcast on the way to work. You work with twelve browser tabs open, Slack pinging, texts coming in. You eat lunch while watching YouTube. You come home exhausted, crash on the couch, and scroll until you fall asleep.

Every moment is filled with input. Every second is claimed by something. And at the end of the day, you're drained—but you can't point to anything meaningful you actually built.

That's because you spent your attention budget on consumption, not creation. You were busy, but you weren't building.

The old way keeps you reactive. You respond to notifications, follow trends, consume content, and chase dopamine hits. But you never create anything that compounds. You can't multiply what you constantly interrupt.

3. The Genyus Way

"Attention is your first currency."

Quiet millionaires see attention as the budget behind all budgets. They know that where attention flows, energy—and eventually money—follows.

They treat attention like a precious resource. They unsubscribe from chaos. They turn off notifications that don't earn or inspire. They schedule silence as aggressively as meetings. They've learned that protecting focus is cheaper than recovering it.

They understand that your brain has an operating budget every day—and if you overspend it on nonsense, you'll have nothing left for creativity or growth. That's why they call it an energy budget.

Here's the shift: **Old belief:** "I need to stay connected and informed."
New truth: "Most information is noise. I choose signal."

Old belief: "Multitasking makes me more productive."
New truth: "Multitasking makes me mediocre at everything."

Old belief: "I'll miss out if I'm not constantly checking."
New truth: "I'm missing out on my own life by constantly checking."

Quiet millionaires don't try to do everything. They protect their attention so fiercely that they only do what matters. And because they're focused, what they do actually compounds.

They've learned that five minutes of full attention beats two hours of scattered effort. They've learned that your brain has limited processing power—and when you spend it on drama, it can't spend it on design. When you give it to complaints, it can't give it to creativity.

That's why they win. Not because they work harder, but because they work with full attention on the right things.

4. Practical Examples

Let's look at how this plays out in real life.

Morning Routine: The old way is to wake up, grab your phone, and scroll for twenty minutes before you even get out of bed. Your brain is immediately flooded with other people's opinions, problems, and agendas. By the time you start your day, your attention budget is already half-spent. The Genyus way is to start quiet—no screens for thirty minutes. Journal, visualize your goals, move your body, or just sit in silence. You protect your morning attention so you can invest it in what matters.

Workday Interruptions: The old way is constant email alerts and open chat windows. Every ping pulls you out of focus. You think you're being responsive, but you're actually being reactive. The Genyus way is to check messages twice a day—once mid-morning, once mid-afternoon. You batch communication so you can protect long stretches of uninterrupted focus. That's where real work happens.

Negative People: The old way is to argue, explain, and over-engage with people who drain you. You think you're being helpful or standing your ground, but you're actually hemorrhaging attention. The Genyus way is to detach politely and redirect your focus to solutions. You don't ignore people—you just refuse to let them steal your energy.

Content Consumption: The old way is random podcasts, endless news loops, and scrolling through content that makes you feel worse. The Genyus way is to curate an "attention playlist"—books, shows, and creators that raise your frequency. You consume intentionally, not compulsively.

Evening Wind-Down: The old way is to collapse on the couch and scroll until your eyes hurt. You think you're relaxing, but you're actually overstimulating your brain right before sleep. The Genyus way is to set a screen curfew—no phones or screens one hour before bed. Read, stretch, talk to someone you love, or just sit quietly. You protect your sleep by protecting your evening attention.

Every attention leak is a tiny hole in your wealth bucket. Plug them, and suddenly you have more time, energy, and ideas—the real ingredients of freedom.

5. Why This Works

Focus compounds like money. Five minutes of full attention beats two hours of scattered effort.

Your brain has limited processing power. When you spend it on drama, it can't spend it on design. When you give it to complaints, it can't give it to creativity. When you waste it on noise, it has nothing left for signal.

Quiet millionaires win because they keep their mental bandwidth invested in creation, not reaction.

Here's why protecting your attention is so powerful: **It creates clarity.** When you stop filling every moment with input, you finally have space to think. And thinking is where ideas are born. **It builds energy.** Distraction is exhausting. Focus is energizing. When you protect your attention, you feel less drained at the end of the day. **It compounds results.** One focused hour produces more than ten distracted hours. When you protect your attention, your output multiplies. **It restores peace.** Constant stimulation creates constant anxiety. Silence creates calm. And calm is the foundation of every good decision.

The economy of attention is simple: you have a limited supply, and the world has unlimited demand. If you don't guard it, it will be taken from you. But if you protect it, you can invest it in the things that actually build wealth, health, and freedom.

6. Reflection Prompts

Take a moment and answer these questions honestly. Write them down—don't just think about them.

What are three things that drain your attention but give nothing back? These might be apps, people, habits, or environments. Name them. Once you name them, you can start eliminating them.

What activity leaves you feeling mentally full, not empty? This is your signal. This is where your attention should go. It might be reading, creating, building, learning, or connecting deeply with someone you love. Whatever it is, do more of it.

If attention is currency, what's one "investment" that always pays peace or progress? This is your anchor. When you feel scattered, return to this. It's your North Star for where your attention should flow.

7. Actions You Can Take

Don't just read this and move on. Take action today.

Action Step: The One-Week Attention Audit

For the next seven days, track where your attention goes. You don't need a fancy system—just a notes app or a piece of paper. At the end of each day, write down three attention leaks—things that wasted your focus—and one focus upgrade that could replace each leak.

Here are some examples to get you started: If your leak is scrolling social media first thing in the morning, your focus upgrade could be reading fifteen pages of a book instead. If your leak is complaining about a problem, your focus upgrade could be spending that time planning a fix. If your leak is background TV while you're trying to work, your focus upgrade could be lo-fi music and a timer for focused work blocks.

Tiny upgrades done daily rewire your brain for clarity—and clarity is profit.

Here are some other specific actions you can take right now: Turn off one unnecessary notification today. Just one. Tomorrow, turn off another. Delete one app that steals your attention without giving anything back. Schedule one daily focus hour—sixty minutes with no interruptions, no phone, no distractions. Protect it like a meeting with your future self. Create a morning routine that doesn't include screens for the first thirty minutes. Start your day with intention, not reaction. Set a screen curfew—no phones or devices one hour before bed. Let your brain rest so it can create tomorrow.

Pick one. Start today. Watch what happens when you stop spending your attention and start investing it.

8. Closing Thought

"Every time you say no to distraction, you say yes to freedom."

Gen Xers already know how to focus—we just forgot. We grew up in a world that demanded our full attention. We know what it's like to commit to one thing at a time. We know what it's like to wait, to be patient, to be present.

Now we just need to remember.

Your attention is your fortune. Protect it like gold. Invest it like seed money. And watch everything else—your energy, your income, your peace—grow from that one decision.

The world will always demand your attention. But only you can decide where it goes.

CHEAT CODE 6: The Self-Duplication Playbook

Build systems that earn while you sleep.

1. Opening Story

I was invited to a barbeque with a lot of people I really didn't know too well. I'm one of those Gen X loners who questions the wisdom of attending one of these gatherings the moment I walk into the yard and hear the chatter of people talking about a dozen topics that I probably have no interest in. Yeah, I know, I never got over my social awkwardness.

Eventually I found myself by the coolers selecting a soda when a gentleman strikes up a conversation. I put on my best "tell me more about your life" face and listen. He tells me all about himself, the business he owns, the vacations he's planning, the car he drives, and did I mention the business he owns? I did? Good, because he mentioned it about three times within a ten-minute monologue of over-sharing.

Carpet cleaning was his game. He'd been doing it for ten years. He seemed very happy.

When he finally took a breath I asked him how many trucks he had running. He looked at me quizzically as if he'd already answered the question five times. "It's just me," he said. "I run that truck from sun up to sun down."

I nodded approvingly, all the while thinking to myself: he actually doesn't own a business. He owns a job.

I mentioned this point in Track One. Owning your own job is perfectly fine. In fact, it's often preferable to working the same hours and letting someone else make all the money off of the labor you are putting in. But there is a big distinction between owning a business and owning a job.

This is how you can tell the difference. Ask yourself this question: **If I don't get up in the morning, do I still make money?**

If the answer is no, then what you own is a job. If you still make money regardless of whether you are in bed, at an amusement park, or playing video games, then you own a business—because a business is an entity comprised of systems, resources, and pro-cedures that generates revenue for the business owner.

It's important that you keep this mentality in mind as you progress towards retirement, because what you want is to attach as many money or revenue-generating opportunities to your life as possi-ble. This includes the topic of assets.

The simplest explanation for what an asset is: **something that puts money into your pocket.** If it takes money out of your pocket, then it's a liability. When it comes to things like houses, some people classify them as assets, but technically they take money out of your pocket every month in the form of mortgages, insurance, maintenance costs, etc. So, I like to include a third category of "investment" to the mix—which is something we are putting money towards that we anticipate will one day give us a return on our investment.

The carpet cleaner at the barbeque was working hard. No question. But he was trading hours for dollars. And hours are the one thing you can never get back.

That conversation stuck with me because it highlighted something I see all the time: people confusing motion with progress. They're busy, they're hustling, they're grinding—but they're not building anything that works without them.

Quiet millionaires think differently. They don't just work hard—they work once and get paid repeatedly. They build systems that duplicate their effort. They create assets that generate income whether they show up or not.

That's the difference between being self-employed and being free.

2. The Old Way

Most of us were taught that hard work equals success:

"Work hard and you'll get ahead."
"The harder you work, the more you'll earn."

And that's true—to a point. Hard work matters. But hard work alone will never make you wealthy. Because there's a ceiling on how many hours you can work. There's a limit to how much one person can do.

The old way looks like this: You trade your time for money. You show up, you get paid. You don't show up, you don't get paid. You might be self-employed, you might even call yourself a business owner, but if the business stops when you stop, you don't own a business—you own a job.

You're the bottleneck. Every dollar depends on you. Every client depends on you. Every decision depends on you. And if you get sick, take a vacation, or just need a break? The money stops.

That's not freedom. That's just self-imposed employment with extra stress.

The old way keeps you trapped in the time-for-money exchange. You might make good money, but you're still trading your most valuable resource—your time—for every dollar. And time is the one thing you can never get back.

3. The Genyus Way

"Work once, get paid repeatedly."

Quiet millionaires understand that true wealth comes from dupli-cation, not repetition. They build systems that work without them. They create assets that generate income while they sleep. They duplicate their effort so they're not the bottleneck.

They ask themselves: **"How can I do this once and get paid for it forever?"**

That's the mindset shift. Instead of trading time for money, they invest time into building systems that generate money. Instead of being the worker, they become the architect.

Here's the shift: **Old belief:** "I have to work hard to make money." **New truth:** "I have to work smart to build systems that make money."

Old belief: "If I'm not working, I'm not earning." **New truth:** "If I'm always working, I'm never building."

Old belief: "My income depends on my hours." **New truth:** "My income depends on my systems."

Quiet millionaires don't just hustle harder—they build smarter. They create assets that compound. They duplicate themselves so their income isn't tied to their presence.

That's how you go from owning a job to owning a life.

4. Twelve Ways to Duplicate Yourself

Let's get practical. Here are twelve ways to build systems that earn while you sleep. These aren't theories—they're proven paths to self-duplication. Pick one, start small, and build from there.

1. Digital Products

Create something once, sell it forever. This could be an eBook, a course, a template, a guide, a checklist, or a toolkit. The beauty of digital products is that they cost nothing to duplicate. You create it once, and it can generate income for years. If you're a hair stylist, create a guide on at-home hair care. If you're a coach, create a workbook. If you're a designer, create templates. Whatever expertise you have, package it and sell it while you sleep.

2. Automated Services

Build a service that runs without you. This means hiring people, creating systems, and documenting processes so the business operates whether you're there or not. The carpet cleaner could have hired two more technicians, bought two more trucks, and tripled his income without tripling his hours. That's duplication. You're not doing more work—you're building a system that works without you.

3. Affiliate Marketing

Recommend products you already use and earn a commission when people buy through your link. No inventory, no customer service, no fulfillment. You create content once—a blog post, a video, a social media post—and it generates passive income every time someone clicks and buys. If you're already recommending products to friends, why not get paid for it?

4. Rental Income

Buy assets that other people pay to use. This could be real estate, equipment, vehicles, or even storage space. The asset works for you. You own it, someone else uses it, and you collect the income. A rental property generates income every month whether you're awake or asleep. That's duplication.

5. Subscription Models

Turn one-time sales into recurring revenue. Instead of selling a service once, offer a subscription. Instead of one payment, you get paid every month. This could be a membership site, a monthly coaching program, a subscription box, or ongoing access to your expertise. Recurring revenue is predictable revenue—and predictable revenue is freedom.

6. Licensing Your Work

Create something once and let other people pay to use it. This could be photography, music, designs, software, or intellectual property. You own it, they license it, and you get paid every time it's used. Stock photography is a perfect example—take a photo once, sell it hundreds of times.

7. YouTube or Podcast Ad Revenue

Create content that generates ad revenue long after you publish it. A YouTube video you made two years ago can still be earning money today. A podcast episode can generate sponsorship income for years. You create it once, and it works for you forever. The key is consistency—build a library of content that compounds over time.

8. Print on Demand

Design it once, sell it forever—without inventory or shipping. You create a design for t-shirts, mugs, posters, or phone cases. When someone orders, the product is printed and shipped automatically. You never touch it. You just collect the profit. Platforms like Printful, Redbubble, and Teespring handle everything. You just design and market.

9. Investing in Index Funds or Dividend Stocks

Put your money to work so it earns while you sleep. Index funds grow over time with the market. Dividend stocks pay you quarterly just for owning them. You're not trading time for money—you're letting your money duplicate itself. The earlier you start, the more it compounds.

10. Create a Course or Coaching Program

Package your expertise into a repeatable system. Record your knowledge once and sell it to hundreds or thousands of people. You're not trading hours for dollars anymore—you're duplicating your teaching. One course can generate income for years. One coaching framework can serve clients without you being in every session.

11. Build an Email List and Monetize It

Your email list is an asset. Every subscriber is a potential customer. Build the list once, nurture it with valuable content, and monetize it with offers, affiliate links, or your own products. An email you write once can generate sales for months. That's duplication.

12. Royalties from Creative Work

Write a book, create music, design software, or produce art that generates royalties. You create it once, and you get paid every time someone buys it, streams it, or uses it. Musicians earn royalties every time their song plays. Authors earn royalties every time their book sells. Create once, earn forever.

5. Why This Works

Self-duplication works because it breaks the time-for-money trap. When you duplicate yourself, your income is no longer limited by your hours. You're not the bottleneck anymore. Your systems, your assets, your content—they work for you.

Here's why self-duplication is so powerful: **It creates leverage.** One effort generates multiple returns. You work once and get paid repeatedly. **It builds freedom.** Your income isn't tied to your presence. You can take a vacation, spend time with family, or pursue other projects—and the money still comes in. **It compounds over time.** Every asset you build adds to your income stream. One digital product might earn $500 a month. Ten products earn $5,000 a month. That's compounding. **It creates security.** Multiple income streams mean you're not dependent on one source. If one stream slows down, the others keep flowing.

Quiet millionaires don't just work hard—they build systems that work for them. That's how they go from busy to wealthy. That's how they go from owning a job to owning a life.

6. Reflection Prompts

Take a moment and answer these questions honestly. Write them down—don't just think about them.

If you stopped working tomorrow, how long would your income last? This question reveals whether you own a business or a job. If the income stops when you stop, you're trading time for money. If it continues, you've built duplication.

What skill, knowledge, or asset could you package once and sell repeatedly? This is your duplication opportunity. What do you already know that others would pay to learn? What do you already do that could be systematized?

What's one system you could build this month that earns without your constant presence? Start small. Pick one duplication method from the list above. Build it. Launch it. Let it work for you.

7. Actions You Can Take

Don't just read this and move on. Take action today.

Action Step: Pick One Duplication Method and Start This Week

Choose one method from the twelve above. Just one. Don't try to do them all at once. Pick the one that feels most aligned with your skills, interests, and current situation. Then take the first step this week.

Here are some examples to get you started: If you choose digital products, outline your first eBook or guide this week. What problem can you solve? What knowledge can you share? If you choose affiliate marketing, sign up for one affiliate program and create one piece of content recommending a product you already use. If you choose print on demand, create one design and upload it to a platform like Redbubble or Printful. If you choose investing, open a brokerage account and invest your first $100 in an index fund. If you choose a course or coaching program, outline the framework you would teach. What's the transformation you help people achieve?

The key is to start. Duplication doesn't happen overnight, but it also doesn't happen if you never begin. Take the first step this week. Build momentum. Let the system start working for you.

Here are some other specific actions you can take right now: Audit your current income. How much of it is active versus passive? Write down one skill or piece of knowledge you have that others would pay for. Research one platform that supports your chosen duplication method. Set aside two hours this week to build your first duplicatable asset. Tell one person about your duplication goal. Accountability creates momentum.

Pick one. Start today. Your future self will thank you.

8. Closing Thought

"You'll never get rich trading hours for dollars. But you can get wealthy building systems that work without you."

The carpet cleaner at the barbeque was working hard. But he was still trading time for money. He was still the bottleneck. He was still one injury, one illness, one vacation away from zero income.

You don't have to live that way.

You can build systems that earn while you sleep. You can create assets that generate income whether you show up or not. You can duplicate yourself so your income isn't tied to your hours.

That's not a fantasy. That's a choice. And it starts with one decision: to stop trading time for money and start building systems that work for you.

Pick one duplication method. Start this week. Build your first system. And watch what happens when you're no longer the bottleneck.

Freedom isn't found in working harder. It's found in building smarter.

CHEAT CODE 7: The Entropy Principle
Chaos creates opportunity for those who bring order.

1. Opening Story

Most of us Gen Xers are very familiar with the concept of entropy, even if we don't recognize it by name. Entropy, also known as the 2nd Law of Thermodynamics, is the concept that the universe is in a constant state of moving towards chaos unless energy is put into the system to create order.

Most of us encountered entropy on Saturday mornings after our cartoons, Soul Train, and American Bandstand were off and we wanted to go outside to play with friends. Our desires were immediately met with our parents saying, "Are your chores done?"

We knew that if we wanted to ask our parents for anything, our best chance of them saying yes rested in being able to confirm that the bedrooms were cleaned, the dishes washed, the bathrooms scrubbed when they asked us that gateway-to-freedom and life-outside-with-our-friends question.

And why were the rooms a mess, the dishes dirty, and the bathrooms unkept in the first place? Entropy. Without the energy of keeping these systems up, they lead to a state of chaos.

And believe it or not, mastering this concept could put many thousands of dollars in your pocket when used to your advantage.

Here's what I mean: Everything in life naturally moves toward disorder. Your house gets messy. Your car gets dirty. Your yard gets overgrown. Your finances get complicated. Your business processes get inefficient. Your health deteriorates without maintenance. This isn't a moral failing—it's physics.

But here's the opportunity: **Most people resist entropy in their own lives but ignore it everywhere else.** They let their businesses drift into chaos. They let their systems break down. They let their properties decay. They let their finances spiral out of control.

And that's where you come in.

I learned this lesson the hard way—or rather, the profitable way—when I bought my first rental property. It was a foreclosure, and it was a disaster. The previous owner had let entropy take over completely. The yard was a jungle. The interior was trashed. The systems were broken. It was chaos.

But I saw something different. I saw order waiting to happen. I saw value hidden under the mess. I saw an opportunity that most people would walk away from because they couldn't see past the entropy.

I spent three months putting energy into that system—cleaning, repairing, organizing, restoring. I fought entropy with intention and effort. And when I was done, the property was worth $40,000 more than I paid for it. I didn't create value out of thin air—I created order out of chaos. And the market rewarded me for it.

That's the Entropy Principle: **Chaos is expensive for those who live in it, but profitable for those who fix it.**

Quiet millionaires understand this deeply. They don't run from entropy—they run toward it. They see disorder as opportunity. They know that wherever there's chaos, there's a chance to create value by bringing order.

And the best part? Entropy is everywhere. Which means opportunity is everywhere.

2. The Old Way

Most of us were taught to avoid problems:

"Stay away from messy situations."
"Don't buy anything that needs work."
"Avoid chaos at all costs."

We were taught that problems are bad. That disorder is something to fear. That the safest path is the cleanest path.

So we avoid the fixer-upper house. We avoid the struggling business. We avoid the complicated situation. We walk away from anything that looks like it needs too much work.

The old way looks like this: You only want things that are already perfect. You pay premium prices for turnkey solutions. You avoid anything that requires effort to fix. You see chaos and think "problem." You see disorder and think "risk." You see entropy and run the other way.

But here's what you miss: **The premium you pay for perfection is the profit someone else made by fixing the chaos.**

When you buy the move-in-ready house, you're paying for someone else's effort to fight entropy. When you hire the expensive consultant, you're paying for someone else's ability to bring order to your chaos. When you buy the established business, you're paying for someone else's work to build systems that resist entropy.

The old way keeps you comfortable, but it keeps you broke. Because you're always paying other people to solve entropy instead of profiting from it yourself.

3. The Genyus Way

"Chaos is just order waiting for energy."

Quiet millionaires see entropy differently. They don't avoid it—they seek it out. They understand that disorder is where the deals are. They know that chaos creates discounts. They've learned that the bigger the mess, the bigger the opportunity—if you're willing to put in the work.

They ask themselves: **"Where is entropy creating a discount I can profit from?"**

That's the mindset shift. Instead of paying for perfection, they buy the chaos and create the order. Instead of avoiding problems, they solve problems and capture the value. Instead of running from entropy, they run toward it with a plan.

Here's the shift: **Old belief:** "I should avoid messy situations."
New truth: "Messy situations are where the money is."

Old belief: "Problems are expensive."
New truth: "Problems are expensive for those who live in them, profitable for those who solve them."

Old belief: "I need everything to be perfect before I start."
New truth: "Perfection is expensive. I profit from imperfection."

Quiet millionaires understand that every system naturally drifts toward chaos. Businesses get inefficient. Properties decay. Processes break down. Relationships deteriorate. Health declines. Finances get messy.

But they also understand that **whoever brings order to chaos captures the value.**

That's why they buy the distressed property and renovate it. That's why they acquire the struggling business and fix the systems. That's why they offer services that solve other people's entropy problems. That's why they build businesses around bringing order to chaos.

They're not smarter or luckier—they're just willing to do what most people avoid.

4. Practical Examples

Let's look at how the Entropy Principle creates real income opportunities.

Real Estate Renovation: Buy a property that's been neglected. The yard is overgrown, the paint is peeling, the systems are broken. Most buyers walk away because they see too much work. But you see a discount. You buy it below market value, invest energy and capital into restoring order, and sell it or rent it for significantly more. You didn't create value—you revealed it by fighting entropy.

Flipping Items: Go to estate sales, thrift stores, or online marketplaces and find items that are dirty, disorganized, or poorly presented. Buy them cheap, clean them up, photograph them well, write compelling descriptions, and resell them for profit. The item didn't change—you just brought order to how it was presented. That order has value.

Business Process Consulting: Most businesses drift into inefficiency over time. Their processes get bloated, their systems get complicated, their workflows get chaotic. Offer to come in and streamline their operations. Audit their processes, eliminate waste, create order. Companies will pay you thousands to fight their entropy because they can't see it themselves—they're too close to the chaos.

Digital Decluttering Services: People's digital lives are a mess. Overflowing inboxes, disorganized files, forgotten subscriptions, cluttered cloud storage. Offer a service that brings order to their digital chaos. Organize their files, clean their inbox, cancel unused subscriptions, set up systems that maintain order. This is pure entropy work—and people will pay for it.

Estate Cleanouts: When someone passes away or moves, their belongings become entropy—chaos that needs to be dealt with. Offer estate cleanout services. Sort, organize, donate, sell, or dispose of items. Families will pay you to bring order to an overwhelming situation. And often, you'll find valuable items in the chaos that you can resell for additional profit.

Car Detailing: Cars naturally get dirty and disorganized. Most people let entropy build up until their car is a mess. Offer detailing services that restore order. Clean, vacuum, polish, organize. You're not changing the car—you're fighting entropy. And people will pay $100-$300 for a few hours of your work because they value the order you create.

Financial Organization: Most people's finances are chaotic. Multiple accounts, forgotten subscriptions, disorganized records, no budget, no plan. Offer financial organization services. Help them consolidate accounts, track spending, create budgets, set up automated systems. You're bringing order to financial entropy—and that's worth thousands to someone who's overwhelmed.

Yard Maintenance: Yards drift toward chaos naturally. Grass grows, weeds spread, leaves pile up, branches fall. Offer regular maintenance services that keep entropy at bay. You're not doing anything complicated—you're just consistently applying energy to maintain order. And property owners will pay you monthly for that peace of mind.

Every single one of these opportunities exists because of entropy. The universe naturally creates disorder. You profit by creating order.

5. Why This Works

The Entropy Principle works because it's based on a fundamental law of physics. Everything naturally moves toward disorder. That's not going to change. Which means the opportunity to profit from bringing order will never go away.

Here's why this principle is so powerful: **Entropy is constant.** Disorder never stops. Which means the demand for order never stops. You're not chasing trends—you're working with a permanent force of nature. **Most people avoid chaos.** Which means less competition for you. While everyone else is paying premium prices for perfection, you're buying chaos at a discount and creating your own profit margin. **The value is immediate and visible.** When you bring order to chaos, people can see the difference. The messy house becomes beautiful. The disorganized business becomes efficient. The cluttered space becomes peaceful. The transformation is obvious—and that's what people pay for. **It's infinitely scalable.** Entropy exists everywhere, at every level. You can start small—flipping thrift store items—and scale up to renovating properties or consulting for businesses. The principle is the same; only the scale changes.

Quiet millionaires build entire fortunes on this principle. They buy distressed assets, fix them, and sell them. They acquire struggling businesses, optimize them, and profit. They offer services that solve entropy problems for people who are overwhelmed by chaos.

They're not doing anything magical. They're just willing to bring order where others see only mess.

6. Reflection Prompts

Take a moment and answer these questions honestly. Write them down—don't just think about them.

Where do you see entropy in your own life that you've been avoiding? This could be a cluttered garage, disorganized finances, an inefficient work process, or a neglected property. Identify it. Because if you can't fight entropy in your own life, you can't profit from it in others' lives.

What skills do you have that could bring order to someone else's chaos? Can you organize? Clean? Repair? Streamline? Optimize? Simplify? These are entropy-fighting skills—and they're valuable.

What "messy" opportunity have you been avoiding because it seemed like too much work? That avoidance is costing you money. The work is where the profit is. The mess is where the margin is. What would change if you stopped avoiding chaos and started seeing it as opportunity?

7. Actions You Can Take

Don't just read this and move on. Take action today.

Action Step: Find One Entropy Opportunity This Week

Look around your life, your neighborhood, your network, and identify one place where entropy has created an opportunity. It doesn't have to be big. Start small. The goal is to practice seeing chaos as profit potential.

Here are some examples to get you started: Find one item in your home you no longer use. Clean it, photograph it well, and sell it online for more than you think it's worth. You're practicing fighting entropy for profit. Offer to organize a friend's garage or closet for $50. You're practicing bringing order to chaos and getting paid for it. Look for a neglected property in your area. Research what it would take to restore it and what it would be worth after. You're practicing seeing value hidden in entropy. Audit one process in your own work or business. Identify inefficiencies and streamline them. You're practicing fighting entropy in systems. Offer to help a family member or friend with a task they've been avoiding be-cause it's overwhelming—cleaning out a storage unit, organizing paperwork, decluttering a room. Do it for free this time, but notice how much value you create. That's your future income stream.

The key is to start seeing entropy everywhere—and seeing oppor-tunity in it. Once you train your brain to recognize chaos as profit potential, you'll never run out of ways to make money.

Here are some other specific actions you can take right now: Walk through your home and identify three areas where entropy has taken over. Pick one and restore order today. Visit a thrift store or estate sale and find one undervalued item. Buy it, clean it up, and resell it. Research one service business built around fighting entropy—cleaning, organizing, repair, maintenance. Study their pricing and process. Make a list of five skills you have that could bring order to chaos. These are your entropy-fighting superpowers. Identify one person in your network who's overwhelmed by chaos in some area of their life. Offer to help.

Pick one. Start today. Train your brain to see opportunity in disorder.

8. Closing Thought

"The universe creates chaos. You create profit by bringing order."

Entropy is not your enemy—it's your business partner. It's constantly creating opportunities for you to add value. It's constantly creating discounts for you to capture. It's constantly creating problems for you to solve.

Most people see chaos and run. You see chaos and recognize it for what it is: order waiting for energy.

And whoever brings the energy captures the value.

That foreclosure property? It's not a disaster—it's a discount. That cluttered garage? It's not a mess—it's a paycheck. That inefficient business process? It's not a problem—it's a consulting opportunity. That overgrown yard? It's not neglect—it's recurring revenue.

Entropy is everywhere. Which means opportunity is everywhere.

The question is: Are you willing to do the work that most people avoid?

Because if you are, you'll never run out of ways to make money. The universe is literally creating opportunities for you every single day. All you have to do is bring order to the chaos.

Start small. Fight entropy in one area. Capture the value. Then do it again. And again. And watch what happens when you stop avoiding the mess and start profiting from it.

Chaos isn't the problem. Chaos is the opportunity.

CHEAT CODE 8: Plugging the Leak
You can't fill a bucket with holes in it.

1. Opening Story

Gen X grew up watching TV shows like Three's Company, Good Times, Archie Bunker, and the list goes on. One of the common traits among our favorite characters was that they were just normal people, living a normal life, and that included just getting by when it came to paying bills.

It's like they were trying to program us to expect to struggle and simply hand over our paychecks to several bill-collecting entities, because, you know, that's life. Cue the laugh track.

As we grew up, we saw debt as just another part of life. For crying out loud, Wilma Flintstone and Betty Rubble used to jokingly yell "CHARGE IT!" as their battle cry before going to the stores to spend money. Suffice it to say, the best, most responsible examples of how to manage wealth were not laid before our eyes as youngsters.

I remember getting my first credit card at nineteen. It came in the mail—unsolicited—with a $500 limit and a letter congratulating me on being "pre-approved." I felt like I'd won something. Like someone had finally recognized that I was an adult worthy of credit.

I used it immediately. Bought things I didn't need with money I didn't have. And when the bill came, I paid the minimum. Because that's what you do, right? That's what everyone does. That's what the TV families did. You charge it, you pay a little each month, and life goes on.

Except life didn't just go on. The balance grew. The interest compounded. And before I knew it, that $500 limit was maxed out, and I was paying $25 a month just to stay current—most of it going to interest, barely touching the principal.

I wasn't building wealth. I was bleeding it. Every single month.

That credit card was a leak. And I didn't even know it.

Here's what I've learned since then: **Most people focus on earning more money, but they ignore the leaks.** They work harder, get raises, start side hustles—and wonder why they're still broke. It's because their bucket has holes in it.

You can pour all the water you want into a bucket with holes, but it's never going to fill up. You have to plug the leaks first.

That's what this track is about. Not earning more—though that matters. Not investing better—though that matters too. This is about finding the leaks in your financial life and plugging them. Because until you do, nothing else works.

Quiet millionaires understand this deeply. They don't just focus on income. They obsess over leaks. They know that a dollar saved from a leak is worth more than a dollar earned, because you don't have to work for it—you just have to stop losing it.

So let's find your leaks. And let's plug them.

2. The Old Way

Most of us were taught that debt is normal:

"Everyone has a car payment."
"You need credit cards for emergencies."
"Student loans are good debt."
"A mortgage is just part of homeownership."
"You have to spend money to make money."

We were taught that monthly payments are just a fact of life. That everyone carries balances. That debt is a tool. That as long as you can make the minimum payment, you're fine.

So we accumulate leaks without even realizing it. A car payment here. A credit card balance there. A subscription we forgot about. A gym membership we never use. A storage unit full of stuff we don't need. A phone plan that's twice what we should be paying.

Each one seems small. Manageable. Not worth worrying about.

But they add up. And they compound. And before you know it, you're working just to cover the leaks. Your paycheck comes in and immediately flows out to a dozen different places. You're running on a treadmill, working harder and harder but never getting ahead.

The old way normalizes this. It tells you that everyone lives this way. That it's just part of being an adult. That you'll always have bills, always have debt, always be one paycheck away from disaster.

But that's not true. That's just what happens when you ignore the leaks.

3. The Genyus Way

"Plug the leaks first. Then focus on filling the bucket."

Quiet millionaires don't accept leaks as normal. They hunt them down ruthlessly. They understand that every dollar leaking out is a dollar that could be building wealth instead. They know that plugging a $200-a-month leak is the same as giving yourself a $2,400-a-year raise—except you don't have to work for it.

They ask themselves: **"Where is my money going that isn't serving my future?"**

That's the mindset shift. Instead of accepting monthly payments as inevitable, they question every single one. Instead of carrying debt because "everyone does," they eliminate it aggressively. Instead of letting subscriptions and expenses run on autopilot, they audit everything regularly.

Here's the shift: **Old belief:** "Everyone has debt. It's normal."
New truth: "Debt is a leak. I plug leaks."

Old belief: "As long as I can make the payments, I'm fine."
New truth: "Every payment is money that could be building wealth instead."

Old belief: "I need to earn more to get ahead."
New truth: "I need to plug the leaks first, then earning more actually matters."

Quiet millionaires understand that wealth isn't just about what you make—it's about what you keep. And you can't keep anything if your bucket is full of holes.

So they plug the leaks. Every single one. And then—and only then—do they focus on filling the bucket.

4. The Seven Biggest Leaks (And How to Plug Them)

Let's identify the most common leaks and how to fix them. These are the holes that are draining your wealth right now.

Leak #1: High-Interest Debt

This is the biggest leak for most people. Credit card debt at 18% or 20% interest is like trying to fill a bucket with a gaping hole in the bottom. You can pour money in all day, but most of it's going to interest, not principal. Here's how to plug it: List all your debts from highest interest rate to lowest. Pay minimum payments on everything except the highest-rate debt. Throw every extra dollar at that one until it's gone. Then move to the next. This is the avalanche method, and it saves you the most money. If you have multiple high-interest debts, consider a balance transfer to a 0% APR card to stop the bleeding while you pay it down. Or look into a personal loan at a lower rate to consolidate and reduce the interest. The goal is simple: stop paying 18% interest. It's a leak you can't afford.

Leak #2: Car Payments

The average car payment in America is over $700 a month. That's $8,400 a year. Over five years, that's $42,000—plus interest. And at the end, you own a depreciating asset worth half what you paid. This is a massive leak. Here's how to plug it: If you have a car payment, make it your mission to pay it off as fast as possible. Then, keep driving that car and redirect the payment amount into savings. When you need your next car, pay cash. Buy a reliable used car for $8,000 or $10,000 instead of financing a $40,000 new one. Yes, it's less flashy. But that $700 a month you're not paying? That's $8,400 a year you can invest. Over twenty years at 10% returns, that's over $500,000. Your car payment is costing you half a million dollars in future wealth. Plug the leak.

Leak #3: Subscriptions You Don't Use

Streaming services, gym memberships, software subscriptions, meal kits, subscription boxes—they're everywhere. And they're designed to be forgettable. You sign up, they auto-renew, and you forget you're paying. The average person has subscriptions they don't even remember. Here's how to plug it: Go through your bank and credit card statements for the last three months. Highlight every recurring charge. Ask yourself: "Am I actively using this? Does it add enough value to justify the cost?" Cancel anything you're not using at least weekly. For the ones you keep, see if you can downgrade to a cheaper tier or share with family to split the cost. Even if you only find $50 a month in forgotten subscriptions, that's $600 a year. That's a Roth IRA contribution. That's an emergency fund. That's wealth you're currently leaking away.

Leak #4: Eating Out Too Often

Food is one of the biggest budget leaks for most people. Not groceries—eating out. Lunch at work, dinner because you're too tired to cook, coffee runs, weekend brunches. It adds up fast. The average American spends over $3,000 a year on dining out. Many spend much more. Here's how to plug it: You don't have to stop eating out completely. Just be intentional. Set a monthly dining-out budget and stick to it. Meal prep on Sundays so you have lunch ready for the week. Make coffee at home and bring it with you. Cook dinner at home four nights a week instead of two.

If you can cut your dining-out spending in half, you'll save $1,500 a year. That's another Roth IRA contribution. That's another income stream you could start. That's wealth instead of convenience.

Leak #5: Paying for Convenience

Delivery fees, expedited shipping, convenience store markups, ATM fees, late fees, overdraft fees—these are all convenience leaks. Individually, they're small. But they add up to hundreds or thousands of dollars a year. Here's how to plug it: Plan ahead. Buy groceries instead of using delivery services. Order online with free shipping instead of paying for expedited. Use your bank's ATM to avoid fees. Set up autopay to avoid late fees. Keep a buffer in your checking account to avoid overdraft fees. These leaks are 100% avoidable. They're just laziness tax. Stop paying it. Redirect that money toward your future instead.

Leak #6: Lifestyle Inflation

This is the sneakiest leak. You get a raise, so you upgrade your apartment. You get a bonus, so you buy a nicer car. You get a promotion, so you start shopping at more expensive stores. Your income goes up, but so do your expenses—so you never actually get ahead. Here's how to plug it: When your income increases, don't increase your lifestyle. Keep living on your old income and direct the difference toward wealth-building. Got a $5,000 raise? That's $416 a month. Don't upgrade your life—invest it. Max out your Roth IRA. Build your emergency fund. Start a side business. Pay off debt. The gap between what you earn and what you spend is where wealth is built. Don't let lifestyle inflation close that gap.

Leak #7: Not Shopping Around

Most people set up their bills once and never look at them again. Insurance, phone plans, internet, utilities—they just auto-renew year after year, often at increasing rates. Meanwhile, competitors are offering better deals to new customers. Here's how to plug it: Once a year, audit all your recurring bills. Call your providers and ask for a better rate. If they won't budge, switch to a competitor. Shop around for car insurance, home insurance, phone plans, internet. You can often save $50 to $200 a month just by making a few phone calls. That's $600 to $2,400 a year. For an hour of work. This is one of the highest-return activities you can do. Yet most people never do it. Don't be most people. Plug the leak.

5. Why This Works

Plugging leaks works because it's immediate and permanent. When you eliminate a $200-a-month leak, you've just given yourself a $2,400-a-year raise. Forever. You don't have to negotiate with a boss. You don't have to work extra hours. You just stop losing money.

Here's why this principle is so powerful: **It's in your control.** You can't always control your income, but you can always control your leaks. You have 100% power to plug them. **It's immediate.** The moment you cancel a subscription or pay off a debt, the leak stops. You see results right away. **It's permanent.** Once you plug a leak, it stays plugged. That money is yours to keep, invest, or build with—forever. **It compounds.** Every leak you plug frees up money that can be redirected toward wealth-building. That money then grows and compounds over time. A $200-a-month leak plugged and invested at 10% for twenty years becomes over $150,000.

Quiet millionaires don't just earn more—they keep more. They plug every leak, no matter how small. Because they understand that wealth is built in the gap between earning and spending. And the wider that gap, the faster wealth grows.

6. Reflection Prompts

Take a moment and answer these questions honestly. Write them down—don't just think about them.

What's the biggest financial leak in your life right now? Be honest. Is it debt? Car payments? Eating out? Subscriptions? Identify it. Because you can't plug a leak you won't acknowledge.

How much money is leaking out of your life every month that isn't serving your future? Add it up. Debt payments, unused subscriptions, convenience fees, dining out. What's the total? That number is your opportunity. That's how much wealth you could be building instead.

If you plugged your three biggest leaks, what would you do with that money? Would you invest it? Build an emergency fund? Start a business? Pay off debt faster? Get clear on this. Because when you know what you're building toward, it's easier to plug the leaks.

7. Actions You Can Take

Don't just read this and move on. Take action today.

Action Step: The 30-Day Leak Audit

For the next thirty days, track every single dollar you spend. Every coffee, every subscription, every bill, every purchase. Write it down or use an app. At the end of thirty days, review your spending and identify your leaks.

Here's what to look for: Recurring charges you forgot about or don't use. High-interest debt that's costing you hundreds in interest every month. Convenience spending that could easily be eliminated with a little planning. Lifestyle expenses that aren't adding real value to your life. Bills you've never shopped around for or negotiated.

Pick your three biggest leaks and commit to plugging them within the next sixty days. Not all of them—just three. Make them specific and actionable.

Here are some examples to get you started: If high-interest debt is your biggest leak, create a payoff plan and commit to paying an extra $200 a month toward the highest-rate debt. If car payments are draining you, commit to paying off your car within the next twelve months, then never financing a car again. If subscriptions are leaking money, cancel everything you're not using weekly and redirect that money to your Roth IRA. If eating out is your leak, commit to cooking at home four nights a week and packing lunch three days a week. If you haven't shopped around for insurance in years, spend one afternoon getting quotes and switch to save $100 a month.

The key is action. Identify the leaks. Plug them. Redirect the money toward wealth-building. Watch what happens.

Here are some other specific actions you can take right now: Log into your bank account and review the last three months of transactions. Highlight every recurring charge. Call your insurance company, phone provider, and internet provider. Ask for a better rate. If they say no, get quotes from competitors. Cancel one sub-scription today. Right now. Even if it's just $10 a month. Practice plugging a leak. Calculate how much interest you're paying on all your debts this year. Let that number motivate you to attack the debt aggressively. Set up a separate savings account called "Plugged Leaks." Every time you eliminate a recurring expense, redirect that exact amount into this account automatically. Watch it grow.

Pick three leaks. Plug them this month. Redirect the money. Build wealth instead of bleeding it.

8. Closing Thought

"You can't fill a bucket with holes in it. Plug the leaks first."

We grew up watching TV families struggle with money and laugh about it. We were taught that debt is normal, that monthly payments are just part of life, that everyone lives paycheck to paycheck.

But that's not true. That's just what happens when you accept the leaks.

Quiet millionaires don't accept leaks. They hunt them down. They plug them. They refuse to let their hard-earned money drain away to interest, subscriptions, convenience fees, and lifestyle inflation.

They understand something simple but powerful: **A dollar saved from a leak is a dollar that can build wealth forever.**

You don't need to earn six figures to build wealth. You don't need to get lucky or inherit money or stumble into the perfect investment. You just need to plug the leaks and redirect that money toward your future.

That $200 a month you're losing to leaks? Over twenty years at 10% returns, that's over $150,000. That's not small money. That's life-changing money. That's freedom money.

But only if you plug the leak.

So stop accepting debt as normal. Stop letting subscriptions run on autopilot. Stop paying convenience fees and lifestyle inflation taxes. Stop bleeding wealth.

Find the leaks. Plug them. Redirect the money. Build wealth instead.

It's not sexy. It's not exciting. It won't make you feel like JR Ewing or the people on the soap operas. But it works.

And twenty years from now, when your friends are still struggling with the same leaks they have today, you'll be financially free. Because you plugged the holes and filled the bucket.

Start today. Find one leak. Plug it. Then find another.

That's how quiet millionaires are built. One plugged leak at a time.

CHEAT CODE 9: 401K Mysteries Solved
Simplifying what everyone else seems to already know

1. Opening Story

Twenty-year high school reunion. A sports bar in our hometown that used to be a corn field back in the day. The smell of wings and beer, the sound of cR&B and alternative rock playing too loud, and a table full of classmates I hadn't seen since we walked across that graduation stage in 1994.

We'd all taken different paths.

Mike went military—twenty years in the Air Force, retired at 42 with a pension that pays him for life. He was talking about his next chapter, maybe teaching, maybe consulting, but the point was clear: he didn't *have* to work. His pension covered his basics. Everything else was gravy.

Carlos went the municipal route—firefighter for the city. Twenty-five years in, pension locked, healthcare covered. He was talking about retiring at 50 and spending his days fishing and coaching Little League.

Then there was me.

Corporate America. Climbed the ladder. Changed companies a few times chasing better titles and bigger paychecks. Contributed to my 401(k) when I could. Did everything I was supposed to do.

But sitting at that table, listening to Mike and Carlos talk about their pensions, their guaranteed monthly income, their healthcare coverage—I felt exposed. Vulnerable. Like I'd been playing a completely different game and didn't realize it until now.

We were all the same age. But they had *certainty*. They had *security*. They had systems that would take care of them for the rest of their lives.

And I had... a 401(k) balance that felt a lot smaller than it should be, and a nagging feeling that I was on my own.

Because I was.

I didn't go the government route. I didn't serve. I didn't lock in a pension. I chose the corporate path—the path that promised opportunity and upward mobility but delivered layoffs, mergers, and the constant anxiety of knowing that my retirement was entirely on me.

No one was going to send me a check every month for the rest of my life. No one was going to cover my healthcare. No one was going to reward my loyalty with guaranteed income.

I was responsible. Fully. Completely. And sitting at that table, I realized I needed a better plan.

That night, I went home and started researching. Not just how to save more—but how to build a system that could give me the kind of security my friends had, even without a pension. The results were not great. There isn't much good informatoin out there. Don't get me wrong, there are TONS of opinions from people who may or may not be living the success they claim. But that's not what I wanted...no, needed. I needed something proven.

Thankfully, that's when a very dear friend of mine introduced me to his Hybrid 401(k) Strategy. Not only did it work, but it made sense to someone like myself.

It's not a pension. But it's the closest thing you can build on your own. And if you're like me—if you chose the corporate path, if you're on your own, if you don't have a government safety net—this strategy can give you the stability and income you need to retire with confidence.

Let me show you how it works.

2. The Old Way

Most people approach their 401(k) with one of two mindsets:

Mindset 1: "I'll just max it out and hope for the best."

They contribute as much as they can, pick a target-date fund, and hope the market cooperates. They don't think about tax treatment, liquidity, or diversification. They just dump money in and cross their fingers.

Mindset 2: "I'll contribute enough to get the match and that's it."

They see the 401(k) as a checkbox. Get the free money from the employer match, then move on. They don't think strategically about how to maximize compounding, minimize taxes, or build a balanced retirement income system.

Both approaches miss the bigger picture.

The old way treats retirement savings as a single bucket. You put money in, it grows (hopefully), and someday you pull it out and pay taxes on it. It's simple. But it's not optimized.

Here's what the old way misses:

Tax diversification: All your money is in   one tax treatment (pre-tax 401(k)), which means you'll pay ordinary income   tax on every dollar you withdraw in retirement.

Liquidity: Your 401(k) is locked up until   59½. If you need money before then, you're hit with penalties.

Growth potential: Most people play it too   safe in their 401(k), missing out on compounding growth in their peak   earning years.

Behavioral discipline: Without a system,   people contribute inconsistently, miss opportunities to increase savings   with raises, and fail to diversify.

The old way leaves you with a 401(k) balance that might be decent—but it's not optimized for long-term income, tax efficiency, or flexibility.

And when you're competing against friends with pensions, "decent" doesn't feel like enough.

3. The Genyus Way

"Build a three-tiered retirement system that captures guaranteed returns, tax-free compounding, and flexible growth."

The Hybrid 401(k) Strategy isn't about just saving more. It's about building a *system*—a three-tiered approach that maximizes employer match, leverages tax-free compounding, and maintains liquidity.

Think of it like building your own pension. You're creating multiple income streams with different tax treatments and different purposes, all working together to give you stability, growth, and flexibility in retirement.

Here's the framework:

Tier 1: The Guaranteed Return Zone (401(k) Employer Match)

Contribute enough to your 401(k) to capture the full employer match—typically 4% of your salary. This is free money. It's an instant 100% return on investment. You can't beat that anywhere else.

But here's the key: *Invest this money conservatively.* Put it in low-risk, cash-equivalent funds or stable value funds. The goal here isn't growth—it's *capital preservation with guaranteed returns.* You've already doubled your money with the match. Don't risk it chasing higher returns.

Tier 2: The Tax-Free Compounding Zone (Roth IRA)

After you've captured the full employer match, take 80% of your remaining savings capacity and put it into a Roth IRA. For most people aiming to save 10% of their income, this is about 4.8%.

Invest this money in *dividend-producing stocks*—stable, blue-chip companies that pay consistent dividends. Think Coca-Cola, Johnson & Johnson, Procter & Gamble. Companies that have been paying and increasing dividends for decades.

Why? Because dividends in a Roth IRA are *tax-free forever.* They compound tax-free. They grow tax-free. And when you withdraw them in retirement, they're tax-free.

This is your wealth-building engine. This is where compounding does its magic over 20, 30, or 40 years.

Tier 3: The Flexible Growth Zone (Taxable Brokerage Account)

Take the remaining 20% of your savings capacity—about 1.2% of your income—and put it into a taxable brokerage account. Invest this money in *growth stocks*—companies with high growth potential that may not pay dividends but have strong capital appreciation potential.

Why? Because this money is *liquid.* You can access it anytime without penalties. And when you sell, you pay capital gains tax, which is typically lower than ordinary income tax.

This tier gives you flexibility. If you want to retire early, if you have an emergency, if you want to make a big purchase before 59½—this money is available.

The Three-Tiered System in Action:

Tier 1 (401(k) Match): 4% of income   Low-risk funds Guaranteed returns

Tier 2 (Roth IRA): 4.8% of income   Dividend stocks   Tax-free compounding

Tier 3 (Taxable Brokerage): 1.2% of   income   Growth stocks Liquidity and flexibility

Total savings rate: 10% of gross income.

This system gives you:

Capital safety from the matched 401(k)   funds

Tax-free income from Roth IRA dividends

Growth potential from taxable equities

Liquidity for emergencies or early   retirement

Tax diversification across three   different tax treatments

You're not just saving. You're building a system that works like a pension—multiple income streams, tax-efficient, stable, and flexible.

4. The Behavioral Enhancements That Make It Work

The strategy is only as good as your ability to stick with it. Here are the behavioral rules that make the Hybrid 401(k) Strategy work long-term:

Enhancement 1: Automate Everything (Dollar-Cost Averaging)

Set up automatic contributions to all three tiers. Every paycheck, money flows automatically into your 401(k), your Roth IRA, and your brokerage account. You never see it. You never touch it. It just happens.

This removes emotion from the equation. You're not trying to time the market. You're not second-guessing yourself. You're just consistently investing, month after month, year after year. This is dollar-cost averaging, and it smooths out market volatility while building wealth steadily.

Enhancement 2: The Raise Rule

Every time you get a raise, increase your Roth IRA and brokerage contributions by 5% of that raise. Not all of it—just 5%. You still get to enjoy 95% of your raise, but you're also accelerating your wealth-building.

Example: You get a $5,000 annual raise. That's about $416 a month. Increase your Roth IRA contribution by $21 a month (5% of $416). You barely notice it, but over time, this compounds into serious wealth.

This rule ensures that your savings grow with your income. You're not stuck at the same contribution level for decades. You're scaling up as you earn more.

Enhancement 3: Annual Stock Expansion

Once a year, add one new dividend-producing stock to your Roth IRA. Just one. This gradually diversifies your holdings and reduces risk. Over 20 years, you'll have 20 different dividend-paying stocks—a diversified portfolio that generates consistent, tax-free income.

You don't need to be a stock-picking genius. Just focus on blue-chip dividend aristocrats—companies that have increased their dividends for 25+ consecutive years. These are stable, reliable companies that have weathered recessions, market crashes, and economic upheaval.

Enhancement 4: Adjust Risk with Age

As you get older, gradually shift your Roth IRA holdings from growth-oriented dividend stocks to more conservative, higher-yield dividend stocks. In your 40s and 50s, you can afford more growth. In your 60s, you want more income and stability.

This isn't about timing the market. It's about matching your portfolio to your life stage and risk tolerance.

Enhancement 5: Reinvest and Rebalance Annually

Once a year, review your three tiers. Reinvest all dividends. Rebalance if one tier has grown significantly larger than the others. This keeps your system aligned with your strategy and ensures you're not overexposed to any single asset class or tax treatment.

This annual review takes maybe an hour. But it keeps your system optimized and on track.

5. Why This Works

The Hybrid 401(k) Strategy works because it's built on proven financial principles and human behavior:

It captures guaranteed returns. The employer match is free money—an instant 100% ROI. You're starting from a position of strength.

It leverages tax-free compounding. Roth IRA dividends compound tax-free for decades. This is one of the most powerful wealth-building tools available. Over 30 years, the difference between taxable and tax-free compounding is massive.

It provides liquidity. The taxable brokerage account gives you access to money before 59½ without penalties. This is critical if you want to retire early or need funds for emergencies.

It diversifies tax treatment. You're not putting all your eggs in one tax basket. You have pre-tax money (401(k)), tax-free money (Roth IRA), and taxable money (brokerage). This gives you flexibility in retirement to manage your tax burden strategically.

It's automated. You set it up once, and it runs on autopilot. This removes the emotional decision-making that derails most people's retirement plans.

It scales with your income. The Raise Rule ensures that your savings grow as you earn more. You're not stuck at the same contribution level forever.

It hedges inflation. Dividend-paying stocks tend to increase their dividends over time, which helps your income keep pace with inflation. Your purchasing power is protected.

It's simple. You're not day-trading. You're not chasing hot stocks. You're not trying to time the market. You're just consistently investing in proven assets and letting compounding do the work.

This isn't a get-rich-quick scheme. It's a get-rich-slowly system. And slow and steady wins the retirement race.

6. Reflection Prompts

Before you implement this strategy, answer these questions honestly. Write them down.

Are you currently capturing your full employer 401(k) match? If not, you're leaving free money on the table. This is the first thing to fix. If you are, are you investing it conservatively to protect that guaranteed return?

Do you have a Roth IRA, and are you maximizing contributions? If not, why? The tax-free compounding in a Roth IRA is one of the most powerful wealth-building tools available. If you're not using it, you're missing out.

Do you have a taxable brokerage account for liquidity and flexibility? If not, you're locking all your money away until 59½. What if you want to retire early? What if you need funds before then? Liquidity matters.

When you get a raise, where does that money go? Does it disappear into lifestyle inflation, or are you directing some of it toward your future? The Raise Rule is one of the simplest ways to accelerate wealth-building without feeling the pinch.

Are you investing consistently, or do you try to time the market? Dollar-cost averaging removes emotion and smooths volatility. If you're not automating your investments, you're making it harder than it needs to be.

7. Actions You Can Take

Don't just read this and move on. Take action today.

Action Step: Build Your Three-Tiered System

Here's how to implement the Hybrid 401(k) Strategy step by step:

Step 1: Calculate your target savings rate. Aim for 10% of your gross income. If that feels like too much right now, start with 6% and work your way up. The key is to start.

Step 2: Contribute enough to your 401(k) to capture the full employer match. This is typically 4% of your salary. If your employer matches 6%, contribute 6%. Don't leave free money on the table. Invest this money in a stable value fund, money market fund, or bond fund. The goal is capital preservation, not growth.

Step 3: Open a Roth IRA if you don't already have one. Contribute 80% of your remaining savings capacity to this account. For most people, this is about 4.8% of income, or roughly $400–$500 a month depending on your salary. Invest in dividend-producing stocks. Start with one or two dividend aristocrats—companies like Johnson & Johnson, Coca-Cola, or Procter & Gamble. Add one new stock per year.

Step 4: Open a taxable brokerage account. Contribute the remaining 20% of your savings capacity—about 1.2% of income, or $100–$150 a month. Invest in growth stocks or a low-cost index fund like the S&P 500. This is your liquidity and flexibility fund.

Step 5: Automate all contributions. Set up automatic transfers from your paycheck or checking account to all three accounts. Make it so you never have to think about it. Automation is the key to consistency.

Step 6: Implement the Raise Rule. Next time you get a raise, increase your Roth IRA and brokerage contributions by 5% of that raise. Put it on your calendar. Make it a habit.

Step 7: Schedule an annual review. Once a year, review your three tiers. Reinvest dividends. Rebalance if needed. Add one new dividend stock to your Roth IRA. Adjust risk as you age. This takes an hour and keeps your system optimized.

Here are some other specific actions you can take right now:

Log into your 401(k) account and check your contribution rate. Are you getting the full match? If not, increase your contribution today.

If you don't have a Roth IRA, open one this week. Fidelity, Vanguard, and Schwab all make it easy. It takes 15 minutes.

Research three dividend aristocrat stocks. Read about their history, their dividend track record, and their business model. Pick one and buy your first shares in your Roth IRA.

Calculate 10% of your gross income. Break it down: 4% to 401(k), 4.8% to Roth IRA, 1.2% to brokerage. Write it down. Make it real.

Set up automatic contributions to all three accounts. Make it so you never have.

8. Closing Thought

"You don't need a pension to retire like you have one. You just need a system."

Sitting at that reunion table, listening to my friends talk about their pensions and guaranteed income, I felt like I'd made the wrong choice. Like I'd missed out on something they had figured out.

But here's what I realized later: **They didn't figure anything out. They just chose a path that came with a built-in system.**

Military service comes with a pension. Government work comes with a pension. Corporate America? You're on your own.

But being on your own doesn't mean you're without options. It just means you have to build your own system.

And that's exactly what the Hybrid 401(k) Strategy is—a system you build yourself that works like a pension.

Three tiers. Three tax treatments. Three purposes. All working together to give you stability, growth, and flexibility.

You capture the guaranteed return from your employer match. You build tax-free compounding wealth in your Roth IRA. You maintain liquidity and growth potential in your brokerage account.

It's not complicated. It's just intentional.

Mike has his military pension. Carlos has his firefighter pension. And you? You're building something just as powerful—you're just building it yourself.

Twenty years from now, you'll sit at another reunion table. And when the conversation turns to retirement, you won't feel exposed. You won't feel behind. You won't wonder if you made the wrong choice.

You'll know that you built a system that takes care of you. A system that generates income. A system that gives you options and freedom.

Because you didn't need someone to give you a pension. You built your own.

Start today. Tier 1: capture the match. Tier 2: build tax-free wealth. Tier 3: maintain flexibility.

Automate it. Scale it with raises. Let it compound for decades.

That's how you retire with confidence—even without a pension.

That's how Gen Xers take care of themselves. We always have. We always will.

CHEAT CODE 10: Infinite Liquidity
The Hidden Power of Whole Life Banking

1. Opening Story

Two kids. Same neighborhood. Same high school. Same graduation year. But two completely different financial educations.

Jason came from money. Not flashy money—quiet money. His grandfather owned a manufacturing business. His father was a commercial real estate investor. At family dinners, they didn't talk about sports or politics—they talked about cash flow, leverage, and tax strategy.

When Jason turned 25, his father sat him down and said, "We're going to set up your financial foundation. You're going to fund a Whole Life policy for the next ten years. You won't touch it. You'll just pay the premiums. And when you're 35, you'll have your own bank."

Jason didn't fully understand it at the time. But he trusted his father. So he did it. Every month, like clockwork, premiums went into the policy. He didn't think about it. He just paid it like a bill.

By the time Jason was 35, he had over $400,000 in cash value sitting in that policy. And that's when his father taught him the next lesson: "Now you borrow against it. Buy a rental property. Start a business. Invest in an opportunity. But you never withdraw from it—you borrow against it. The money keeps growing, and you keep using it."

Jason bought his first rental property with a policy loan. Then another. Then he started a side business. Every time he borrowed, he repaid the loan with interest—back to his own policy. He was his own bank. And the cash value kept compounding, year after year, tax-deferred.

By 45, Jason had built a real estate portfolio, owned two businesses, and still had a growing cash value in his Whole Life policy. He was financially free. Not because he earned more than everyone else—but because he had a system.

Then there was me.

I came from a different world. My parents lived paycheck to paycheck. There were no family dinners about cash flow or leverage. There was no grandfather with a manufacturing business. There was no financial foundation being laid for my future.

I worked hard. I earned a decent living. I saved when I could. But I was always one step behind. I didn't have access to capital when opportunities came up. I didn't have a system. I was just grinding, hoping things would work out.

I didn't learn about Whole Life banking until I was in my forties—sitting across from Jason at a coffee shop, listening to him explain how he'd been using his policy as a personal bank for over a decade.

"Wait," I said. "You're telling me you've been borrowing money from yourself, paying yourself back with interest, and the money never stops growing?"

"Exactly," he said. "It's how my family has done it for three generations. It's not a secret. It's just not something most people know about."

I felt that familiar sting—the same one I felt at the reunion when my friends talked about their pensions. The realization that there was a game being played, and I didn't even know the rules.

But here's the thing: **It's not too late to learn the rules. And it's not too late to start playing.**

Whole Life Insurance, when structured correctly, isn't just a death benefit. It's a wealth-building tool. A liquidity engine. A personal banking system that the wealthy have been using for generations.

And if you're willing to learn how it works—and commit to funding it properly—you can build your own bank too.

Let me show you how.

2. The Old Way

Most people think of life insurance in one of two ways:

Way 1: "Life insurance is just a death benefit."

You pay premiums your whole life, and when you die, your family gets a payout. It's protection, not an investment. You never see the money while you're alive. It's just a safety net for your loved ones.

Way 2: "Term life is cheaper, so that's all I need."

Buy term, invest the difference. That's the advice you hear everywhere. Term life is cheaper, so you buy a 20- or 30-year term policy, and you invest the money you save in the stock market. When the term ends, you don't need insurance anymore because you've built wealth elsewhere.

Both approaches miss the hidden power of properly structured Whole Life Insurance.

Here's what the old way misses:

Liquidity: Your money is locked away in retirement accounts or tied up in investments. You can't access it without penalties, taxes, or selling assets.

Compounding continuity: When you withdraw from your investments to use the money, that money stops compounding. You're interrupting the growth.

Tax efficiency: Most investments are taxable. Gains are taxed. Withdrawals are taxed. Dividends are taxed. You're constantly giving a cut to the IRS.

Control: You're dependent on banks for loans. You're dependent on the market for growth. You don't control the system—you're just participating in it.

Legacy wealth: Term life expires. If you outlive the term, there's no death benefit. Your family gets nothing.

The old way treats life insurance as a simple protection product. But the wealthy treat it as a *financial instrument*—a tool for building liquidity, preserving wealth, and creating generational legacy.

And that's the difference between Jason's path and mine.

3. The Genyus Way

"Build your own bank inside a Whole Life policy where funds grow tax-deferred, can be borrowed against at will, and keep compounding even while in use."

This is called the Infinite Banking Concept, or Whole Life Banking. And it's one of the most powerful—and least understood—wealth-building strategies available.

Here's how it works:

Phase 1: The Funding Phase (Years 0–8)

You purchase a properly structured Whole Life Insurance policy—not a standard policy, but one designed to maximize early cash value accumulation. This is critical. Not all Whole Life policies are created equal. You need a policy structured with:

· **High early cash value riders** (Paid-Up Additions or PUA riders)

· **Low death benefit relative to premium** (to avoid Modified Endowment Contract status)

· **Dividend-paying mutual insurance company** (not a publicly traded company)

You pay consistent premiums into this policy for 7–10 years. During this time, you're building cash value. The cash value grows at a guaranteed rate (typically 3–5% annually) plus dividends from the insurance company.

You don't touch it. You don't borrow from it. You just fund it. This is the foundation phase.

Phase 2: The Leverage Phase (After Year 8)

Once your cash value has matured—typically after 7–10 years—you can start borrowing against it. Not *from* it—*against* it.

Here's the key distinction: **When you take a policy loan, you're not withdrawing your cash value. You're borrowing from the insurance company, using your cash value as collateral.**

Your cash value stays in the policy. It continues to grow. It continues to earn dividends. It never stops compounding.

Meanwhile, you have access to liquid capital—tax-free—that you can use for anything:

· Buy a rental property

· Start a business

· Invest in an opportunity

· Pay for a wedding or college tuition

· Cover an emergency

The loan is tax-free because it's technically a loan, not a withdrawal. And because your cash value stays intact, it keeps compounding as if you never touched it.

This is the magic of Whole Life Banking: Your money works in two places at once.

Phase 3: The Recycling Phase (Years 9+)

Here's where the system becomes truly powerful: You repay the loan—with interest—back to the insurance company. But because you're repaying it, you're restoring your borrowing capacity.

Think of it like this: You borrow $100,000 from your policy to buy a rental property. The property generates cash flow. Over the next 5–7 years, you use that cash flow to repay the $100,000 loan plus interest.

Now your borrowing capacity is restored. You can borrow again. Buy another property. Start another business. Invest in another opportunity.

You're recycling your capital. You're using the same dollars over and over again.

And the entire time, your cash value is compounding. Your death benefit is growing. Your policy is building wealth—tax-deferred, guaranteed, and liquid.

This is how the wealthy stay liquid, compound without interruption, and ensure their money never stops working for them.

4. The Three-Phase System in Detail

Let's break down exactly how this works with real numbers.

Example Scenario:

· **Age:** 40

· **Annual Premium:** $25,000

· **Policy Structure:** Whole Life with Paid-Up Additions rider

· **Death Benefit:** $3 million

· **Cash Value After 8 Years:** $500,000

Phase 1: Funding (Years 1–8)

You pay $25,000 per year into the policy. Total premiums paid: $200,000. After 8 years, your cash value is approximately $500,000 (this varies by company and policy structure, but this is a realistic example).

Your cash value has grown faster than your premiums because of:

· Guaranteed growth (3–5% annually)

· Dividends from the insurance company

· Compounding on both

You haven't touched the money. You've just been building your bank.

Phase 2: Leverage (Year 9)

You decide to buy a rental property. The property costs $300,000. Instead of going to a bank for a mortgage, you take a policy loan for $300,000.

Here's what happens:

· Your cash value remains $500,000 (it doesn't decrease)

· The insurance company loans you $300,000 at 5% interest

· Your $500,000 continues earning 4% guaranteed growth plus dividends

· You use the $300,000 to buy the property

The rental property generates $2,000/month in cash flow after expenses. That's $24,000/year.

Phase 3: Recycling (Years 10–16)

You use the rental income to repay the policy loan. At $24,000/year, you repay the $300,000 loan (plus interest) in about 7 years.

Now your borrowing capacity is fully restored. You can borrow $300,000 again. Buy another property. Start a business. Whatever you want.

Meanwhile, your cash value has continued growing. After 16 years (8 years of funding + 8 years of leverage and recycling), your cash value might be $700,000 or more.

And you've used that same $300,000 to build a rental property portfolio, all while your policy kept compounding.

This is Infinite Banking. This is how you become your own bank.

5. Why This Works

The Whole Life Banking strategy works because of several powerful financial principles:

Uninterrupted compounding. When you borrow against your cash value instead of withdrawing it, your money never stops growing. This is the key difference between Whole Life loans and traditional withdrawals. Compound interest is most powerful when it's never interrupted.

Tax efficiency. Your cash value grows tax-deferred. Policy loans are tax-free. Dividends are tax-free (as long as they don't exceed premiums paid). And the death benefit passes to your heirs tax-free. You're building wealth in a tax-sheltered environment.

Guaranteed growth. Unlike the stock market, your cash value has a guaranteed minimum growth rate. You're not subject to market crashes, recessions, or volatility. Your floor is protected.

Liquidity and control. You can access your money anytime, for any reason, without penalties or approval from a bank. You control the system. You decide when to borrow, how much to borrow, and how to repay.

Recycling capital. By repaying your loans, you restore your borrowing capacity. You're using the same dollars over and over again—buying assets, generating income, repaying loans, and borrowing again. This is how you multiply the power of a single dollar.

Legacy wealth. When you die, your heirs receive the death benefit—minus any unpaid loans—tax-free. This creates generational wealth. Your family inherits a tax-free lump sum that can continue the cycle.

This is how wealthy families stay wealthy. They don't just save money. They build systems that allow their money to work in multiple places at once, compound without interruption, and pass tax-free to the next generation.

6. How to Evaluate an Insurance Broker (Critical)

Here's the problem: **Not all insurance agents understand Whole Life Banking.**

Most agents are trained to sell standard Whole Life policies or, more commonly, to push Term Life and tell you to "invest the difference." They don't understand how to structure a policy for maximum cash value accumulation. They don't understand Paid-Up Additions riders. They don't understand the Infinite Banking Concept.

What is a Paid-Up Additions Rider? Good question.

A Paid-Up Additions (PUA) rider is like a turbo-booster for your Whole Life insurance policy's savings account.

Here's how it works:

Normally, when you pay your insurance premium, some of it goes toward the death benefit (the money your family gets when you die) and some goes into a savings account called "cash value" that grows slowly over time.

But with a PUA rider, you're basically saying: "I want to put extra money into my policy, and I want almost all of that extra money to go straight into my cash value savings account—not toward more death benefit."

Think of it like this: Imagine you have a piggy bank that grows bigger every month. Normally it grows a little bit. But with a PUA rider, you're stuffing extra money into that piggy bank so it grows much faster.

Why does this matter?

Because the faster your cash value grows, the sooner you can borrow against it. And the more you have to borrow against, the more money you can use to buy things like rental properties or start businesses—while your cash value keeps growing.

In simple terms: A PUA rider makes your policy's savings account grow faster so you can use it as your own personal bank sooner.

If you work with the wrong agent, you'll end up with a policy that doesn't work for this strategy.

Here's how to evaluate an insurance broker to make sure you're working with someone who actually understands Whole Life Banking:

Red Flag #1: They push Term Life over Whole Life.

If an agent immediately tries to talk you out of Whole Life and into Term Life, they don't understand this strategy. Term Life has its place, but it's not a wealth-building tool. If they can't explain the difference, walk away.

Red Flag #2: They don't mention Paid-Up Additions (PUA) riders.

A properly structured Whole Life policy for banking purposes must include a PUA rider. This is what accelerates early cash value accumulation. If the agent doesn't bring this up, they don't know what they're doing.

Red Flag #3: They focus only on the death benefit.

If the agent is selling Whole Life purely as a death benefit and doesn't talk about cash value, liquidity, or policy loans, they're treating it like a standard insurance product—not a financial instrument.

Red Flag #4: They represent only one company.

Captive agents (agents who work for only one insurance company) are limited in what they can offer. You want an independent agent who can shop multiple mutual insurance companies and find the best policy structure for your needs.

Red Flag #5: They've never heard of "Infinite Banking" or "Bank On Yourself."

If you mention these terms and they look confused, they're not the right agent. You need someone who specializes in this strategy.

Green Flags: What to Look For

They ask about your financial goals, not just your insurance needs. They want to understand how you plan to use the policy—not just sell you coverage.

They explain the difference between standard Whole Life and cash-value-optimized Whole Life. They understand policy design and can customize it for your strategy.

They represent multiple mutual insurance companies. They can compare options and find the best fit for you.

They talk about policy loans, cash value growth, and tax advantages. They understand the wealth-building aspects, not just the death benefit.

They're certified or trained in Infinite Banking or similar strategies. Look for agents who have completed training with organizations like the Infinite Banking Institute or similar.

Questions to Ask a Potential Agent:

1. "Can you structure a Whole Life policy with a Paid-Up Additions rider to maximize early cash value?"

2. "What mutual insurance companies do you work with, and which one would you recommend for my situation?"

3. "How soon can I start taking policy loans, and what's the typical loan interest rate?"

4. "Can you show me illustrations comparing a standard Whole Life policy vs. one optimized for cash value?"

5. "Have you worked with clients who use Whole Life policies for the Infinite Banking strategy?"

If they can't answer these questions confidently, keep looking.

Bottom line: You need a specialist, not a generalist. Don't go to a commercial insurance agent who's going to plug your money into their company's money market schemes. Find an independent agent who understands Whole Life Banking and can design a policy specifically for this purpose.

7. Reflection Prompts

Before you move forward, answer these questions honestly. Write them down.

Do you currently have access to liquid capital when opportunities arise? Or are you locked into retirement accounts, waiting until 59½ to access your money? Liquidity is power. If you don't have it, you're missing opportunities.

When you need money, where do you go? Do you go to a bank and ask for approval? Do you pull from investments and interrupt compounding? Or do you have your own system? If you don't have your own bank, you're dependent on someone else's.

What would it mean for your financial life if you could borrow money, use it to build wealth, and never stop your money from compounding? Think about that. Really think about it. That's the power of Whole Life Banking.

Are you willing to commit to funding a policy for 7–10 years before you start using it? This isn't a quick fix. It's a long-term strategy. But if you're willing to be patient and disciplined, the payoff is massive.

8. Actions You Can Take

Don't just read this and move on. Take action today.

Action Step: Research and Connect with a Qualified Agent

Start by finding an independent insurance agent who specializes in Whole Life Banking or Infinite Banking. Here's how:

Step 1: Search for specialists. Look for agents trained by the Infinite Banking Institute, Nelson Nash Institute, or similar organizations. Search terms like "Infinite Banking specialist [your state]" or "Whole Life cash value expert."

Step 2: Schedule consultations with 2–3 agents. Don't commit to the first person you talk to. Interview multiple agents. Ask the questions listed in the evaluation section. See who understands the strategy best and who you feel most comfortable working with.

Step 3: Request policy illustrations. Ask each agent to provide illustrations showing:

· Cash value growth over 10, 20, and 30 years

· Death benefit growth

· Loan capacity at different time periods

·   Comparison between standard Whole Life and cash-value-optimized Whole Life

Step 4: Compare mutual insurance companies. Ask which companies they recommend and why. Look for companies with strong dividend payment histories—companies like Mass Mutual, Northwestern Mutual, Penn Mutual, or Guardian (these are examples, not endorsements—do your own research).

Step 5: Understand the commitment. Before you sign anything, make sure you understand:

· Annual premium amount

· How long you need to fund the policy before borrowing

· Policy loan interest rates

· How dividends work

· What happens if you miss a premium payment

Step 6: Start small if needed. If $25,000/year feels like too much, start with $10,000 or $15,000. The strategy still works—it just scales with your premium. The key is to start and to be consistent.

Here are some other specific actions you can take right now:

Read *Becoming Your Own Banker* by Nelson Nash. This is the foundational book on Infinite Banking. It's short, clear, and will give you the full framework. You can finish it in a weekend.

Calculate 10–15% of your annual income. This is a reasonable target for annual Whole Life premiums if you're serious about building a personal banking system. If that feels too aggressive, start with 5–7% and scale up over time.

Review your current financial situation. Do you have money sitting in low-interest savings accounts? Money in taxable brokerage accounts that you're not actively using? Consider redirecting some of that capital into a properly structured Whole Life policy.

Talk to someone who's actually using this strategy. If you know anyone in wealthy circles—business owners, real estate investors, financial professionals—ask them if they use Whole Life Banking. You'll be surprised how many quietly do.

Set a 90-day goal. Give yourself 90 days to research, interview agents, review illustrations, and make a decision. Don't rush it, but don't let it drag on forever either. Procrastination costs you years of compounding.

Action Step: Run the Numbers

Before you commit, run your own scenario:

· How much can you afford to contribute annually?

· How long are you willing to fund the policy before you start borrowing?

· What would you use the first policy loan for? (Rental property? Business? Investment?)

· How would you repay the loan? (Rental income? Business profits? Side hustle?)

Write this down. Make it real. If you can see the path, you're more likely to follow it.

Action Step: Commit to the Long Game

This strategy requires patience and discipline. You're not going to see results in Year 1 or Year 2. But by Year 8 or 10, you'll have a powerful financial tool that most people will never understand.

Make a commitment to yourself: "I will fund this policy consistently for the next 10 years. I will not touch it. I will not quit. I will build my own bank."

Write that commitment down. Sign it. Date it. Put it somewhere you'll see it.

Because when you're three years in and it feels like you're just paying premiums with nothing to show for it, you'll need that reminder. You're building a foundation. And foundations take time.

9. Closing Thought

"The wealthy don't just save money. They build systems that allow their money to work in multiple places at once."

Sitting across from Jason that day, listening to him explain how he'd been using his Whole Life policy as a personal bank for over a decade, I felt that familiar sting of being late to the game.

He'd started at 25 because his father taught him. I was learning at 45 because I had to figure it out on my own.

But here's what I realized: **Late is better than never.**

Jason had a 20-year head start. But I still had 20 or 30 years ahead of me. If I started now, I could still build a powerful financial tool. I could still create liquidity. I could still become my own bank.

And so can you.

You didn't grow up with a wealthy family teaching you these strategies. Neither did I. But that doesn't mean we can't learn them now.

Whole Life Banking isn't a secret. It's just not advertised. It's not taught in schools. It's not pushed by financial advisors who make commissions on mutual funds and brokerage accounts.

But it's how wealthy families have preserved and grown wealth for generations.

They build their own banks. They borrow from themselves. They recycle their capital. They keep their money compounding without interruption. And they pass tax-free wealth to the next generation.

You can do the same thing. You just need to start.

Fund the policy. Be patient. Let it mature. Then borrow against it. Use the money to build assets. Repay the loan. Borrow again. Repeat.

That's the cycle. That's the system. That's how you build infinite liquidity.

Jason's father gave him a 20-year head start. But you're giving your future self—and your kids, and your grandkids—a system that will serve them for generations.

You're not just building wealth. You're building a bank. Your bank.

And twenty years from now, when you're sitting across from someone explaining how you've been borrowing from yourself, repaying yourself, and building wealth tax-free for two decades, they'll look at you the way I looked at Jason.

And you'll realize: **You didn't need a wealthy family to teach you. You just needed to be willing to learn.**

Start today. Find a specialist. Fund the policy. Build your bank.

Because the best time to start was twenty years ago.

The second-best time is right now.

WHATEVER

We've Always Figured It Out

Generation X. The forgotten middle child of American generations.

We were too young to be Boomers, too old to be Millennials. We grew up in the gap between the "Me Generation" and the "Me Me Me Generation." And somehow, we ended up being neither.

They called us slackers. They labeled us "X" because they didn't know what else to call us. We didn't fit their mold. We didn't play by their rules. We didn't trust their systems.

And we were right not to.

We watched our parents devote their lives to companies that laid them off without a second thought. We heard about Social Security our entire lives—but always with the caveat that it wouldn't be there for us. We were told to go to college, get a good job, work hard, and everything would work out.

It didn't.

The pension disappeared. The company loyalty was a lie. The social contract was broken before we even entered the workforce.

And yet, here we are. Still standing. Still working. Still figuring it out.

Because that's what we've always done.

The Latch-Key Generation Grows Up

We grew up in a world that required us to be self-reliant from an early age.

We came home to empty houses and let ourselves in with keys tied to shoestrings around our necks. We made our own snacks. We figured out our homework on our own. We watched Saturday morning cartoons until the adults got home, then we went outside and didn't come back until the streetlights came on.

We passed notes in school lockers—folded into intricate triangles—because that was our social media. We recorded songs off the radio onto cassette tapes, timing the record button perfectly to avoid the DJ's voice. We wore acid-wash jeans and thought we looked cool.

We didn't have helicopter parents. We didn't have participation trophies. We didn't have smartphones to call for help.

We just figured it out.

And now, as we stare down retirement, we're being asked to figure it out again.

No one is coming to save us. No pension. No guaranteed income. No system designed to take care of us.

But that's okay. Because we've never needed anyone to save us anyway.

Why This Book Matters

I wrote this book because I'm tired of watching my generation get overlooked, underestimated, and left to fend for ourselves—again.

We're the generation no one seemed to care about. We were too small to matter politically. Too cynical to market to effectively. Too independent to control.

But when there's a problem to solve? When there's a crisis to manage? When someone needs to step up and get things done?

They call on Gen X.

We're the ones who keep things running. We're the middle managers, the small business owners, the ones who show up and do the work without needing constant validation or a parade.

We don't complain. We don't demand. We just handle it.

And now we're being asked to handle our own retirement—with less support, less time, and less margin for error than any generation before us.

But here's what I know about Gen X: **We're resourceful. We're skeptical. We're resilient. And we don't quit.**

We've been taking care of ourselves since we were kids. We've been navigating broken systems our entire adult lives. We've survived recessions, job losses, market crashes, and a pandemic.

And we'll figure out retirement too.

This book isn't about getting rich quick. It's not about complicated investment strategies or financial jargon. It's certainly not about telling you what you should have done twenty years ago.

This book is about giving you some cheat codes—strategies that actually work—so you can build supplemental income streams and retire with dignity, security, and freedom.

Companies that actually offer pensions would have been great. A trust fund would have been better.

But in the absence of these, this book is about introducing you to systems and a mindset that you can start using today.

The Tracks You've Learned

Let's recap what we've covered:

Cheat Code 1: Master This Before You Go Forward – Don't let other people's lack of vision stop you. Pick your people. Speak to their pain. Deliver real solutions.

Cheat Code 2: The Art of Self-Duplication – Work once, get paid repeatedly. Build assets that generate income without your constant presence.

Cheat Code 3: Your Hidden Leverage – You already have skills and knowledge that can be monetized. Stop underestimating what you know.

Cheat Code 4: The $100 Test – Every dollar is an employee. Deploy it wisely, and it works for you forever.

Cheat Code 5: The Economy of Attention – Attention is your first currency. Protect it fiercely. Invest it wisely.

Cheat Code 6: The Self-Duplication Playbook – Twelve concrete methods to create income that doesn't require trading hours for dollars.

Cheat Code 7: The Entropy Principle – Chaos is just order waiting for energy. Bring order to chaos, and you create value—and profit.

Cheat Code 8: Plugging the Leak – Stop the financial bleeding. Every dollar you keep is a dollar that can compound.

Cheat Code 9: 401(k) Mysteries Solved – Build a three-tiered retirement system that captures guaranteed returns, tax-free compounding, and flexible growth.

Cheat Code 10: Infinite Liquidity – Use Whole Life Insurance as a personal banking system to access capital, compound without interruption, and build generational wealth.

These aren't theories. These are strategies people (myself included) use to prepare for the future.

You don't have to implement all of them. You don't have to be perfect. You just need to pick one or two, start today, and stay consistent.

That's how you catch up. That's how you build security. That's how you retire on your terms.

What Happens Next

You have two choices.

Choice 1: Close this book, feel inspired for a day or two, then go back to hoping everything works out.

You can tell yourself you'll start next month. Next year. When things settle down. When you have more time. When you feel more ready.

But here's the truth: You'll never feel ready. There will never be a perfect time. And every month you wait is a month of potential income you're leaving on the table.

Choice 2: Pick one track. Take one action. Start today.

You don't need to overhaul your entire life. You don't need to quit your job or make drastic changes. You just need to start.

Pick one strategy that resonates with you. Maybe it's the 401(k) steps we covered. Maybe it's building a duplicative income stream. Maybe it's plugging one financial leak.

Just pick one. And start.

Take one action this week. Open a Roth IRA. Research a Whole Life Banking specialist. Identify one hidden skill you can monetize. Audit where your attention is going.

One action. This week.

Then next week, take another action. And the week after that, another.

Small, consistent actions compound into massive results.

That's how you build wealth. That's how you catch up. That's how you retire with confidence.

A Personal Thank You

Before I close, I need to thank someone who has been instrumental in helping me understand some of the more complex investment strategies in this book.

C. Blair – thank you for your continued support, friendship, and insights. Your willingness to share your knowledge about advanced financial concepts, tax strategies, and wealth-building systems has been invaluable—not just to me, but to everyone who will benefit from this book. You've been a mentor, a sounding board, and a trusted friend. I'm grateful for you my brother.

And to you, the reader—thank you for trusting me with your time and attention. I know you have a thousand things competing for both. The fact that you made it to the end of this book tells me you're serious about taking control of your financial future.

That's the first step. And it's the most important one.

The Final Word

We're Generation X. The latch-key kids. The slackers who weren't actually slacking.

We've been figuring things out on our own our entire lives. And we're going to figure out retirement too.

Not because someone handed us a system. But because we built one ourselves.

You don't need a pension. You don't need a wealthy family. You don't need to have started twenty years ago.

You just need to start today.

Pick one track. Take one action. Build one income stream.

Then do it again. And again. And again.

Because twenty years from now, you're going to look back at this moment—the moment you decided to stop hoping and start building—and you're going to be grateful you did.

Your future self is counting on you.

We've always figured it out. And we will again.

Let's build something worth retiring to.

Now go. Start today. You've got this.

– A Fellow Gen Xer Who's Still Figuring It Out

www.ingramcontent.com/pod-product-compliance
Lightning Source LLC
Chambersburg PA
CBHW071223090426
42736CB00014B/2958